IN THE TIME OF
THE BUTTERFLIES

Julia Alvarez

AUTHORED by Meghan Joyce
UPDATED AND REVISED by Adam Kissel

COVER DESIGN by Table XI Partners LLC
COVER PHOTO by Olivia Verma and © 2005 GradeSaver, LLC

BOOK DESIGN by Table XI Partners LLC

Published by GradeSaver LLC, www.gradesaver.com

First published in the United States of America by GradeSaver LLC. 2009

GRADESAVER, the GradeSaver logo and the phrase "Getting you the grade
since 1999" are registered trademarks of GradeSaver, LLC

ISBN 978-1-60259-202-5

Printed in the United States of America

For other products and additional information please visit
http://www.gradesaver.com

Table of Contents

Table of Contents

Table of Contents

Biography of Alvarez, Julia (1950-)

Julia Alvarez was born to Dominican parents in New York City in 1950. When she was three months old, her family moved back to the Dominican Republic under the rule of Rafael Trujillo. Her father became involved in a political rebellion, and her family was forced to flee the country in 1960.

Her transition to American life was difficult, but she became an avid reader and dedicated herself to learning English fluently. She was sent to boarding school at the age of 13, and she returned to the Dominican Republic each summer. She graduated from Abbot Academy in 1967 and attended Connecticut College, then transferred to Middlebury College in Vermont in 1969. She earned a Master's degree in creative writing from Syracuse University in 1975.

In the late 1970s, Alvarez worked as a Writer-in-Residence for the Kentucky Arts Commission. Through the 1980s she held various positions at California State College (Fresno); College of the Sequoias in Visalia, California; Mary Williams Elementary School in Wilmington, Delaware; Phillips Andover Academy in Andover, Massachusetts; the University of Vermont; the George Washington University in Washington, D.C.; and the University of Illinois (Urbana). Alvarez's first published work was *The Housekeeping Book* (1984).

Alvarez worked as a professor at Middlebury College from 1988 to 1998, and has been a Writer-in-Residence in the English Department since then. In 1989, Alvarez married Bill Eichner, an ophthalmologist from Nebraska and the father of two daughters from a previous marriage. Her first novel, *How the García Girls Lost Their Accents* (1991), was the first major novel by a Dominican author to be published in English. Alvarez also has written three books of poetry, including *Homecoming* (1991). *In the Time of the Butterflies* (1994) was followed by *¡Yo!*, a sequel to *How the García Girls Lost Their Accents*. Among her many awards, recently she was honored with The F. Scott Fitzgerald Award by Montgomery College (Maryland) on October 17, 2009.

Alvarez and Eichner own La Altagracia, a "sustainable" coffee-bean farm seventeen kilometers west of the small ecotourist city Jarabacoa and seventeen kilometers east of Pico Durate, the highest peak east of the Mississippi River. Proceeds from the sales of coffee support their Foundation Alta Gracia, which funds a school on the farm that helps natives of all ages become literate. In addition the school, also open to foreign students, teaches students about the farm's "sustainable" practices. Alvarez returns to the Dominican Republic and tends the farm.

About In the Time of the Butterflies

In the Time of the Butterflies was published in 1994. It was selected as a Notable Book for 1994 by the American Library Association, and it was also a 1994 Book of the Month Club choice. In 1995, it was a finalist for the National Book Critics Circle Award in fiction, and it was chosen as one of the Best Books for Young Adults by the Young Adult Library Services Association and the American Library Association. The book was made into a film in 2001, directed by Mariano Barroso and starring Salma Hayek as Minerva. Mark Anthony played the role of Lío.

In the Time of the Butterflies is a fictionalized account of the revolutionary activity and personal lives of the Mirabal sisters and their families and compatriots in the Dominican Republic under the Trujillo regime. It is divided into three sections of four chapters each. Each part opens with Dede. Her narration is in the third person whereas the narration of the other sisters is in the first person. Her chapters are divided into two parts: the present (1994) and the past, when her sisters were alive, beginning with 1943. The time frame of the "present" is a span of just one afternoon, during which Dede gives an interview. The interview questions transport Dede (and thus the reader) back in time and into the consciousness of each sister.

Character List

Patria

The oldest of the Mirabal sisters, she is the most religious. At first she planned to enter a convent but then chose to marry Pedrito Gonzales at the age of 16. Her full name is Patria Mercedes Mirabal.

Pedrito Gonzales

Patria's husband, who was incarcerated during the revolution along with their son, Nelson. She thinks of him as animal-like, and his character is inextricably linked to the earth. After Patria's death he is restless until he remarries a young girl.

Nelson

Patria and Pedrito's son, who becomes involved in the revolution and is arrested along with his father.

Noris

Patria's daughter, who comes of age just before her mother is killed.

Raul Ernesto

Patria's youngest son, named after Che Guevara of the Cuban revolution.

Dede

Bélgica Adela "Dedé" Mirabal-Reyes, the second oldest of the Mirabal sisters, and the only one to survive the Trujillo regime. She is married to Jaimito during the action of the story, but the reader learns that they divorced in 1984. They have three sons: Enrique, Rafael, and David.

Jaime Enrique

One of Dede and Jaimito's sons.

Jaime Rafael

One of Dede and Jaimito's sons.

Jaime David

One of Dede and Jaimito's sons.

Minerva

María Argentina Minerva Mirabal, the third Mirabal sister, and the one most wrapped up in the revolution. She and her revolutionary husband, Manolo

Tavarez, have two children: Minou and Manolito.

Manolo

Minerva's husband, who is also imprisoned as a revolutionary. They meet in Jarabacoa while they are both studying law--and while he is engaged to someone else. After Minerva's death, he stays active in the revolution, and he is gunned down.

Minou

Minerva and Manolo's daughter, who lives with Dede in 1994 and has a husband and baby of her own.

Manolito

Minerva and Manolo's son.

Maria Teresa

Antonia María Teresa Mirabal, or "Mate," the youngest Mirabal sister. Her sections of *In the Time of the Butterflies* are narrated in diary form. She is married to Leandro Guzman.

Leandro Guzman Rodriguez

Maria Teresa's husband, whom she met through Minerva and Manolo, and who is also imprisoned as a revolutionary. When they meet, he operates under the codename Palomino and is an engineer working on projects throughout the country. He also makes deliveries between revolutionary cells. After Manolo's death, he becomes a builder in the capital and gets out of politics. He also has remarried and started a new family.

Jaqueline

The daughter of Maria Teresa and Leandro.

Enrique Mirabal

The father of Patria, Dede, Minerva, and Maria Teresa. He drinks often and has an affair with Carmen, a woman on the Mirabal family property, with whom he has children.

The interview woman

This "gringa" woman interviews Dede in 1994, and her questions provoke Dede to retreat into the past and remember the events that led up to her sisters' deaths. She is "such a thin woman with fly-about hair in her face."

Sinita Perozo

Minerva's friend and fellow revolutionary, who first explains to Minerva that Trujillo's regime is evil. When they meet as children, she is "a skinny girl with a sour look on her face and pokey elbows to match." During a performance for Trujillo and his son Ramfis, she comes dangerously close to shooting Trujillo with a bow and arrow.

Sor Milagros

One of the nuns at Inmaculada Concepcion, where the girls go to school.

Lourdes

One of Minerva's friends at Inmaculada Concepcion.

Elsa Sanchez

One of Minerva's friends at Inmaculada Concepcion, who is "pretty in an I-told-you-so way, as if she hadn't expected to turn out pretty and now she had to prove it." She marries a journalist, Roberto Suarez, and they surprise Minerva by refusing to join the revolutionary movement.

Trujillo

Rafael Leonidas Trujillo Molina, the dictator of the Dominican Republic from 1930 until his assassination in 1961. As described by Sinita to Minerva, "Trujillo became president in a sneaky way. First, he was in the army, and all the people who were above him kept disappearing until he was the one right below the head of the whole armed forces."

Sor Asuncion

One of the nuns at Inmaculada Concepcion, who allows Sinita to go to school there for free.

Lina Lovaton

A schoolmate of Minerva, in whom Trujillo takes an interest. She becomes one of his many mistresses. She is "grownup-looking for her age, tall with red-gold hair and her skin like something just this moment coming out of the oven, giving off a warm golden glow."

Ramfis

Rafael Leonidas Ramfis, Trujillo's son, a full colonel in the army since the age of four. When Sinita approaches Trujillo with a bow and arrow during the girls' performance, Ramfis jumps up and breaks her bow.

Tono

A man who works for the Mirabals in their home. He continues to work at the museum in 1994.

Fela

The Mirabals' maid, who continues to work for Dede in 1994. She believes that she can commune with the three dead sisters, and she tells Minou what they say.

Berto

One of the Mirabals' cousins, on whom Maria Teresa has a crush as a young girl.

Raul

One of the Mirabals' cousins and Berto's older brother. Maria Teresa has a crush on both of them as a young girl.

Tia Flor

Berto and Raul's mother and the Mirabal girls' aunt. She is married to Tio Pepe.

Tio Pepe

One of the Mirabals' uncles. He is married to Tia Flor and is the father of Raul and Berto.

Tio Mon

One of the Mirabals' uncles, who lives in La Vega. Minerva lies and says he is sick, and that that is the reason she has been sneaking out of school.

Don Horacio

Elsa's grandfather, who is in trouble with the police. Minerva goes to her first revolutionary meetings at his home with Elsa, Lourdes, and Sinita.

Hilda

A revolutionary orphan with whom Minerva becomes friends while she is at Inmaculada Concepcion. Maria Teresa describes her as wearing "trousers and a beret slanted on her head like she is Michelangelo." The police catch her while she is leaving the convent.

Jaimito

Dede's cousin and husband.

Mario

One of the distributors of Enrique Mirabal's store, who introduces Dede and Minerva to Lio.

Lio

Virgilio Morales, "a tall thin man" with thick, wire-rimmed glasses. When Dede and Minerva meet him, he has just returned from Venezuela, where he earned his medical degree. He asks Minerva to come away with him, and he sends her letters which Enrique Mirabal, her father, keeps from her.

Carmen

The woman with whom Enrique Mirabal has been having an affair and with whom he has other children, including Margarita.

Margarita

The oldest of Carmen's children by Enrique Mirabal. When she visits Patria with a note from Maria Teresa, she has "a sweet, simple face and dark, thick hair held back with bobby pins. The eyes, the brows, the whole look had Mirabal written all over it." She gets her pharmacy degree and supports her younger sisters.

Manuel de Moya

Trujillo's secretary of state, whose real job is to round up young girls for Trujillo to take advantage of. He tries to seduce Minerva at the Discovery Day party.

Don Antonio de la Maza

The governor, who suggests that Minerva allow Trujillo to sleep with her in order to save her father, after Enrique Mirabal is taken to jail. He is "a tall, handsome man with a worried face."

Chea Mirabal

The mother of the Mirabal sisters, who defends her daughters with a passion. She often insists that wherever they go or wherever her husband goes, she is going, too. She dies twenty years after her three daughters. She is unable to read or write, though Maria Teresa teaches her a little.

General Federico Fiallo

A "courtly, white-haired man" at the National Police Headquarters, who interrogates Minerva about Lio and her relationship with him.

Don Anselmo Paulino

Trujillo's right-hand man, called "Magic Eye" because he lost an eye in a knife fight, and his "remaining good eye magically sees what everyone else misses." He roughly interrogates Minerva about Lio at the National Headquarters.

Tio Chiche

Mama's uncle, who knew Trujillo during their early days in the military. She points out this connection to Trujillo in order to try to remain on his good side.

Prieto

The yardboy, who works for the Mirabal household. He betrays them by reporting everything he hears at Security "for a bottle of rum and a couple of pesos."

Eduardo

Manolo's brother.

Padre de Jesus Lopez

Patria's priest, who is "straight out of seminary and brimming with new ideas." He tells her that he, too, is "lost so that I can't show you the way." He becomes involved in the revolution.

Brother Daniel

The speaker at the retreat where Patria goes with other Catholic women when, on the 14th of June, the church is attacked.

Don Bernardo

An old Spaniard who moved to the countryside near Mama's house with his wife Dona Belen from San Cristobal.

Dona Belen

Don Bernardo's wife, whom he takes care of. "Something was wrong with the frail, old woman--she was forgetting the simplest things."

Tinita

Dede's maid, who came to work for her when Jaime David was born.

Dona Leila

Jaimito's mother, who dotes on Dede, her daughter-in-law, so much "that Dede sometimes worried that Leila's five daughters would resent her."

Captain Pena

Victor Alicinio Pen, the head of the northern division of the SIM. He is a very fat man with "sharp, piglike eyes," and a toady of Trujillo. After Pedrito and Nelson are arrested, he takes over their land.

Padre Gabriel

Padre de Jesus' replacement at Patria's church, who speaks of revolution from the pulpit.

Santiclo

The guard at the prison where Minerva and Maria Teresa are held, who brings them things from the outside world and delivers their messages to Patria and Mama, through Margarita. "Santiclo" means "Santa Claus," and it is their code name for him.

Dinorah

One of Minerva's and Maria Teresa's cellmates, who is resentful of the richer women.

Magdalena

One of Minerva's and Maria Teresa's cellmates at the jail, whom Maria Teresa calls "our little birdseed bell." She has a little girl and is "pretty dark with quite a kink in her hair." She tells Maria Teresa about her tragic life story, then tries to kiss her.

Violeta

One of Minerva's and Maria Teresa's cellmates in jail. At the end of one of their group rosaries, she says, "May I never experience all that it is possible to get used to."

Balbina

One of Minerva's and Maria Teresa's cellmates in jail. She is deaf, and Maria Teresa teaches her how to write her name.

Sina

One of Minerva's and Maria Teresa's cellmates in jail. She is educated and leads the revolutionary meetings in the cell along with Minerva. However, Delia reports later that she has left and sought asylum, abandoning the movement.

Delia Santos

One of Minerva's and Maria Teresa's cellmates in jail. She is a doctor, and after they are released, Minerva and Patria visit her to ask about the state of the movement. She sends them to Dr. Pedro Vinas.

Rufino

The driver who is the Mirabal sisters' favorite, who takes them to visit their husbands in prison. He is murdered along with them.

Dr. Pedro Vinas

A urologist in Santiago. Delia tells Minerva and Patria that he is maintaining the revolutionary movement in their area. He is a "genial little man" and explains to Minerva why the uprising of young men failed.

Dona Fefita

Manolo's mother.

Jorge Almonte

The young attendant at El Gallo, where Minerva, Patria, and Maria Teresa stop to buy purses on the way to visit their husbands in Puerto Plata.

Mateo Nunez

One of Dede's visitors, who reports that he was listening to the radio when he heard the crash of the car carrying the bodies of her sisters.

Olga

Dede's friend in 1994, with whom she tries to "catch up with what our children call *the modern times.*"

Doroteo

Minou's husband.

Sonia

Maria Teresa's roommate at Dona Hita's. She is also a university student and involved in the revolution.

Dona Hita

Maria Teresa's and Sonia's landlady while they store deliveries from Leandro, still attending classes at the university. She assumes that they are prostitutes and he is their pimp.

The young soldier

On their trip to visit their husbands in Puerto Plata, the sisters and Rufino pick up the young soldier on the side of the road. He is on his way back to Puerto Plata after a three-night furlough to meet his newborn son in Tamboril.

Major Themes

Authoritarianism

Much of the action of *In the Time of the Butterflies* occurs during Rafael Trujillo's dictatorship in the Dominican Republic. The novel portrays many instances of how the authoritarian state permeates life for the Mirabel sisters and the other characters. For instance, they must watch what they say since there are spies hiding outside their house. Even those citizens who are not suspected rebels are afraid to speak openly, since they cannot trust their own neighbors. In the first chapter, before the Mirabel family comes under any suspicion, their relaxing evening outdoors is ruined when Papa accidentally says Trujillo's name in a less than flattering way. All of a sudden, "the dark fills with spies who are paid to hear things and report them down at Security."

The authoritarian regime of Trujillo is linked to other dictatorships by Maria Teresa in Chapter 7, when she describes the march that she and the other women must participate in before the start of classes: "It looked like the newsreels of Hitler and the Italian one with the name that sounds like fettuccine," namely, Mussolini. In Chapter 12, the theme of authoritarianism is clear when Minerva and Dede are brought into the police station in Monte Cristi. Minerva mentions that Captain Pena has given them permission to travel there, but a veiled threat is perceived in the officer who is questioning them: "The paroxysm of blinking made me pity the poor man. His own terror was a window that opened onto the rotten weakness at the heart of Trujillo's system." Though Minerva recognizes that the fear instilled in all the officers of the authoritarian regime is ultimately a "weakness," for now it is what holds the regime in power.

Courage vs. Cowardice

Courage is valued among the characters, and they display it in varying amounts. The sisters are all aware of their cowardice as they perceive it, and while they sometimes fight for courage, in some cases they simply accept their cowardice. Dede in particular struggles with her cowardice. She acknowledges that it is a factor that prevents her from joining her sisters in their rebellious activities. She is afraid of losing her marriage and is afraid of losing her sisters. She does show courage, however, when she lies and says she is Minerva Mirabel.

Similarly, at the end of Chapter 9, when Dede lies in bed tempted to "just let go," she means that she is tempted to stop trying to maintain her sanity. She talks herself out of it, however, thinking, "Courage! It was the first time she had used that word to herself and understood exactly what it meant." For Dede, courage means staying strong for herself and her family instead of selfishly running away.

Entrapment

Under the reign of Trujillo, the entire country is trapped. The sisters also feel trapped by the expected course of their lives, including boarding school and then marriage, as well as by their religious and familial duties. The feeling of entrapment is expressed by Patria in Chapter 4 when she describes her birth: the midwife "lowered my arms the way you fold in a captive bird's wings so it doesn't hurt itself trying to fly."

Minerva, too, feels trapped, and in Chapter 2 her situation is extended to the entire country. She considers herself trapped at home, so she views going to Inmaculada Concepción as a kind of escape. She sees her situation mirrored in that of the rabbits in their pens, but she realizes that she is not actually like a rabbit when the rabbit that she tries to let free refuses to leave the cage. She realizes, "I'd just left a small cage to go into a bigger one, the size of our whole country." (This point reflects the authoritarianism of Trujillo's reign.)

In the epilogue, the theme of entrapment appears in Dede's reaction to the telegram that Mama shows her on the morning after the girls' death. The telegram says that there has been a car accident and that they should go to the hospital in Santiago, which suggests that the girls were alive and merely injured. When she says, "my heart in my rib cage was a bird that suddenly began to sing. Hope!" the reader understands that her heart, her love for them, despairs in its entrapment inside her body, a "cage," from which certain feelings and thoughts are not allowed to extend. She has been trapped with her own fear. The reader sees in this metaphor the conceit of a cage around the whole nation of the Dominican Republic.

Heaven and Earth

Especially for Patria, who is more in touch with her religion than the other sisters, there is a deeply felt gulf between the divine and the human, between God's perfection and earthly existence. The distinction is especially apparent in her view of Pedrito, whom she often compares to an animal and whom she calls "my earthly groom." When he proposes, he pours a handful of dirt into her hand. This earth gives palpable meaning to her decision to get married to a man instead of figuratively to God as a nun.

When her house is burned down and Nelson and Pedrito are taken away by the police, Patria has a breakdown on her mother's lawn. She tears up the ground in her hands and begins praying the Credo—with Dede's help. In her earthly suffering she calls upon God to provide a link between heaven and earth.

Weaving and Thread

Throughout the novel, all of the sisters use the conceit of life having strings or thoughts that get knotted and must be sorted out, or strings that provide connections which bind people together. For instance, when Patria loses her unborn child, she "went over and over my life to this point, complicating the threads with my fingers, knotting everything," confused about how this tragedy happened. Also, when Dede remembers watching her sisters as they approached her house, she says, "It was as if the three fates were approaching, their scissors poised to snip the knot that was keeping Dede's life from falling apart."

The imagery of woven threads as thoughts appears again in Chapter 6 as Minerva struggles with decisions about where her life should go: "Back and forth my mind went, weaving a yes by night and unraveling it by day to a no." (This is also a reference to Penelope, the wife of Odysseus, who kept putting off her suitors by never finishing her weaving because every night she would undo the work she had done by day.) The yes-or-no question is whether she loves Lio; she cannot decide on this important life-changing question. The threads of her decision seem to fit together at night, but she feels torn during the day. Ultimately, the decision is made for her when he decides to go to asylum.

In Chapter 11, the symbol of threads as connections extends to both a personal level and a national level. When Maria Teresa discusses with Magdalena the connections between people, they decide, "There *is* something deeper. Sometimes I really feel it in here, especially late at night, a current going among us, like an invisible needle stitching us together into the glorious, free nation we are becoming."

In Chapter 12, Minerva tries to get her old self back: "And so the struggle with her began. The struggle to get my old self back from her. Late in the night, I'd lie in bed, thinking, You must gather up the broken threads and tie them together." Somehow the threads of life are worse than just being untangled and dissociated from one another; they are broken. She is trying to reinvigorate the "calm, courageous compañera" whom Manolo married.

The sisters also keep their lives together by literally using thread in their dressmaking business. "We couldn't sleep nights, so we sewed. Sometimes Patria started a rosary, and we all joined in, stitching and praying so as not to let our minds roam." Focusing on physical threads keeps them from dwelling on the distressing threads of their lives.

Trujillo and God

As the Mirabel sisters grow up, it becomes clear that the Trujillo reign permeates their lives. His authoritarian rule, with spies everywhere, suggests that he is trying to assume the role of a terrible God, always watching and ready to punish. In fact, a portrait of El Jefe is hung next to one of Jesus in the entryway of Mama's house. In Chapter 4, while Patria lies beside Minerva in the hammock, they look at the pictures of Jesus and El Jefe side by side. Minerva notes, "They're a pair, aren't they?" This inspires Patria to remember the real difference between divine mercy and justice, on the one hand, and Trujillo's rule, on the other. She asks why God would allow their country to suffer so much at the hands of Trujillo. Yet, when she looks up to challenge the picture of Jesus, "the two faces had merged!" This experience points out the godlike role that Trujillo has assumed Trujillo has taken up the rule of this part of the earth.

Later, Patria even finds herself praying to the portrait of Trujillo, offering herself as a sacrificial lamb in place of her sisters, their husbands, and her own husband. Moreover, Trujillo has created a slogan for himself, "Dios y Trujillo," meaning "God and Trujillo." With this slogan he suggests that God is on his side and has approved of his power. He practically deifies himself in the minds of his subjects, like so many dictators before him.

A similar merging of Trujillo with something of divinity occurs in Chapter 6. The paper fans, which the girls received at the party thrown by Trujillo, have the Virgencita on one side and Trujillo on the other. The combination bothers Minerva: "Sometimes it was El Jefe's probing eyes, sometimes it was the Virgin's pretty face I couldn't stand to look at."

In Chapter 10, Patria remembers the portraits of Jesus and Trujillo side by side and says, "Maybe because I was used to the Good Shepherd and Trujillo side by side in the old house, I caught myself praying a little greeting as I walked by." She wants her family back from Trujillo, and "prayer was the only way I knew to ask." Finally, however, Patria feels the distinction when she arrives at the capital for the release of Nelson. She feels no kinship toward the man—quite the opposite. "The more I tried to concentrate on the good side of him, the more I saw a vain, greedy, unredeemed creature. Maybe the evil one had become flesh like Jesus!"

Women in Politics and Public Life

The sisters often struggle with their perceived role as traditional women who do not take part in politics and public life. In the first chapter, Minerva's frustration is apparent when Mama comments, "Just what we need, skirts in the law!" Minerva argues, however, "It is just what this country needs ... It's about time we women had a voice in running our country."

Similarly in Chapter 4, Patria worries about Minerva getting worked up about the government. She says to her little sister, "It's a dirty business, you're right. That's why we women shouldn't get involved." The argument here is that it may be better to preserve one's innocence and integrity by avoiding politics. Minerva again argues, however, on the basis of an equality principle: "women had to come out of the dark ages."

Speaking to the female interviewer, Dede addresses a similar theme: "'Back in those days, we women followed our husbands.' Such a silly excuse. After all, look at Minerva. 'Let's put it this way,' Dede adds. '*I* followed my husband. *I* didn't get involved.'" She is aware that she is using tradition as an excuse for not having supported her sisters, something for which she still feels guilty.

Glossary of Terms

bandidos
outlaws, bandits

barrio
a division of a city

bruit
to spread a rumor

brujo
sorcerer

cacao
a small, tropical tree cultivated for its seeds, which are the source of chocolate

calmante
a drug used as a tranquilizer to calm the nerves

ceiba
a silk-cotton tree

cortege
a ceremonial procession

gavilleros
the Dominican word for rural bandits

guayabera
a sport shirt or lightweight jacket

hellion
a disorderly or mischievous person

la bendicion
"the blessing," a way to say goodbye

m'ija
a combination of the words "mi hija," meaning "my daughter"

mantilla

a lace or silk scarf worn over the head and shoulders, often over a high comb

mariposas

butterflies, the nickname of the Mirabal sisters as revolutionaries, since it was Minerva's codename

novios

boyfriends

pastelitos

savory pastries

patriomonio

heritage; patrimony

pega palo

stick glue

sancocho

a traditional Dominican soup

sarampion

measles

tutumpotes

members of the old ruling families

yucca

a plant with sword-shaped leaves and clusters of waxy, white flowers, native to warm regions in America

Short Summary

In the Time of the Butterflies is divided into three sections of four chapters each. Each part opens with Dede in third-person narration whereas the narration is given in the first person for the other sisters. Dede's chapters are divided into two parts: 1994 (the present) and the past, when her sisters were alive, beginning with 1943. The time frame of the "present" is a span of one afternoon, in which Dede gives an interview. But the interviewer's questions transport Dede, and the reader, back in time and into the consciousnesses of the sisters.

Part I

Dede begins an interview with a woman at around three o'clock. It is 1994. When Dede asks her what she wants to know, the interviewer answers, "Tell me all of it." Dede is transported back to 1943, to "a clear moonlit night before the future began." The whole family is out in the front yard under the anacahuita tree, relaxing and telling stories.

In 1938, Patria and Minerva go to Inmaculada Concepcion as boarding students. Minerva meets Sinita Perozo, who tells her how Trujillo destroyed her family—killing her uncles, her father, and her brother. Minerva considers, for the first time, that Trujillo is not the saint he makes himself out to be. This realization is driven home when in 1941, her friend Lina Lovaton is chosen to be one of Trujillo's mistresses, destroying her chance at having a fulfilling life. Minerva and her friends are chosen to give a recitation performance for Trujillo at the centennial celebration, but it ends disastrously when Sinita breaks from the script and walks toward Trujillo's chair, taking aim at him.

Maria Teresa has received a diary from Minerva for her First Communion. Patria has gotten married and given birth to two children, Noris and Nelson, and is pregnant with a third. Maria Teresa begins school at Inmaculada Concepcion, where she chooses to lie for Minerva, who has been sneaking out of school to meet secretly with her friends at Don Horacio's house. One of those friends, Hilda, hides at Inmaculada Concepcion, pretending to be a student, but soon she is captured by guards. In July, Minerva graduates and Patria miscarries, losing her son.

In 1946, Patria is 22 years old and, despite always believing she would end up becoming a nun, has chosen to marry Pedrito Gonzales. She is worried about Minerva, who is speaking out against the government. In worrying about Minerva's loss of faith, she herself begins to struggle with her faith. After the miscarriage of Patria's third child, Chea Mirabal decides to take all her daughters on a pilgrimage to Higuey, where it is revealed that Enrique Mirabal is unfaithful to her.

Part II

Back in the present, in 1994, Dede considers that Fela, their longtime servant, thinks that she is possessed by the spirits of the dead Mirabal sisters. The interviewer reminds her about Lio Morales, whom Dede and Minerva met one summer and subsequently invited to play volleyball at Tio Pepe's. When a newspaper that reports that Lio is "a communist, a subversive," Mama becomes upset that she has been letting him spend time at their home. Although she denies being in love with him, Minerva continues to see him—on double dates with Jaimito and Dede. On the night that Jaimito proposes to Dede, Lio gives her a letter to deliver to Minerva, asking Minerva to go into exile with him and his comrades. Dede decides that she will not expose her sister to that danger, so she burns the letter in the lamp.

After graduating from Inmaculada Concepcion, Minerva has been living at home for a few years. She accidentally discovers Carmen, the woman with whom her father has been having an affair, and her four half-sisters. She also discovers four letters from Lio, which her father has been hiding from her. The family is invited to a Discovery Day dance at one of Trujillo's palaces; Manuel de Moya tries to seduce Minerva, and when Trujillo touches her inappropriately, she slaps the dictator in the face. When he pulls her inappropriately close, thrusting at her in a vulgar way, she slaps his face. A rainstorm begins, and the Mirabals escape; but on the ride home, Minerva realizes that she has put the letters from Lio in the pocket of the lining of her purse, which she left at the palace. Enrique Mirabal is sent to the capital for "questioning," and while he is there Minerva brings money to his illegitimate family. Minerva and Chea Mirabal go to the capital to petition for Papa's release. He is released after three weeks, but he has gone insane. In their meeting with Trujillo, Minerva makes a bet with the dictator; she wins, and he allows her to study law.

Maria Teresa has a new journal, which is another gift from Minerva. Enrique Mirabal has passed away, and Maria Teresa mourns his death, but she also has developed crushes on both of her cousins, Raul and Berto. On July 3, Maria Teresa graduates from Inmaculada Concepcion, and in September, she joins Minerva at the university in the capital, and they are roommates. Minerva marries Manolo in 1955, so she moves in with him. Soon, she gives birth to Minou, and in 1957, they move to Monte Cristi.

Trujillo plays a terrible trick on Minerva by not actually granting her a license to practice law; her diploma is useless. Maria Teresa helps Minerva set up her new home in Monte Cristi. She accidentally intercepts a delivery of guns from Leandro, codename Palomino, to the house. Manolo and Minerva explain about the national underground that is forming. Maria Teresa joins them and begins to fall in love with Leandro, whom she marries on Valentine's Day, 1958.

It is now 1959 and Patria's children, Nelson and Noris, have grown up. They all live in Pedrito's great-grandfather's house. Minerva and Manolo visit from Monte Cristi every week; they meet on Patria and Pedrito's land with many other revolutionaries.

This situation gives Nelson the chance to get involved when he is home from school. He reports back to her that the revolutionaries are expecting an invasion by the liberators from Cuba.

Though she is pregnant with Raul Ernesto, Patria decides to go on a retreat with Padre de Jesus and the Salcedo group to Constanza. On the fourteenth of June, the mountainside is bombed. The first wave of the liberating invasion is the target; six days later the second wave is intercepted and also defeated. Padre de Jesus changes the name of the retreat group to Accion Clero-Cultural, or ACC. Though Pedrito protests at first, the Fourteenth of June Movement is founded in Patria and Pedrito's home.

Part III

In the afternoon in 1994, Dede says goodbye to the interviewer just as Minou arrives from Fela's. Back in 1960, Dede has become solitary and feels that Jaimito has become a "bossy, old-fashioned macho" who doesn't notice her unhappiness. Her sisters come to ask her to join their revolutionary cell, and Dede silently decides to leave Jaimito. She is about to ask the priest for advice, but when she realizes that Padre de Jesus is "one of them," she becomes afraid he will convince her to join the revolution, so she flees. Jaimito has left her with his sons, but Manolo convinces them to reconcile and take a vacation together. The next week, Leandro, Pedrito, and Nelson are arrested, and Patria's home has been burned to the ground. Minerva has tuberculosis, but she and Manolo are also arrested before she can get treatment. Dede and Jaimito are able to rebuild some strength in their marriage in their effort to save her sisters.

For three months, Patria stays at her mother's house suffering without her son, husband, or Minerva. Soon, Maria Teresa is also arrested. The Catholic Church speaks out against the regime, and the regime fights back by finding ways to dissuade people from attending church. Through Margarita, one of Enrique Mirabal's illegitimate daughters, Patria and Chea are able to communicate with Minerva and Maria Teresa in La Victoria prison. Captain Pena comes to Chea Mirabal's house with visiting passes, reporting that Nelson might be released with the next round of pardons. But Minerva and Maria Teresa have refused their own pardons. On the next Tuesday, they drive to the capital to pick up Nelson.

In jail at La Victoria, Maria Teresa writes in a smuggled notebook from Carmen's cousin Santiclo, who is one of the guards at La Victoria. On April 11, Maria Teresa is taken to La 40 and whipped in front of Leandro, to try to convince him to do a job for Trujillo, though it is not described what the job is. It works; Leandro cries out, "I'll do it! I'll do it!" On Monday, May 23, Maria Teresa and Minerva are arraigned and sentenced to five years in prison at a "joke of a trial," having no legal representation. The Organization of American States (OAS) is coming to investigate the political prisoners' situation, and Minerva urges Maria Teresa to share with the OAS the incident she has written down. After her ten-minute session in the visitors' hall with seven members of the committee, Maria Teresa lets the letter containing the statement written by Minerva and Sina and signed "The Fourteenth of June Movement" fall out of her braid, and the young commissioner leading her out picks it up. However, she does not let drop the letter with her own personal account. On August 7, Maria Teresa reports that she and Minerva will be released the next day along with the other female political prisoners.

Minerva and Maria Teresa have been released but are now on house arrest. To make money, they start up a specialty business of making children's christening gowns. In prison, Manolo's spirits are crushed when a group of young men is caught distributing revolutionary leaflets in Santiago. Delia Santos tells Minerva to visit Dr. Pedro Vinas, who explains that the "gringos" are helping with the revolution. Manolo fears, however, that they will also take over the country. Minerva loses the house she owns with Manolo, and Dede helps her organize and clean it out. The next Thursday, while they are on the way to visit their husbands, Captain Pena tells them that Manolo and Leandro are being transferred to Puerto Plata, nearer to where the sisters live. On November 25, on the way to Puerto Plata, the sisters' driver, Rufino, decides to stop and pick up a young soldier who is hitchhiking.

The sisters stop at a store called El Gallo on the way to Puerto Plata to buy sewing supplies for their company. The salesclerk, Jorge Almonte, recognizes them and gives Minerva a written warning to "Avoid the pass." But there is nothing to be done, so they keep driving. Nevertheless, they safely arrive at Puerto Plata and visit Leandro and Manolo, who asks Minerva not to drive back that night. After failing to get in touch with their mother by phone, they decide to head home.

Quotes and Analysis

"A chill goes through her, for she feels it in her bones, the future is now beginning. By the time it is over, it will be the past, and she doesn't want to be the only one left to tell their story."

Chapter 1, page 10

Dede feels this chill as her family moves inside from under the anacahuita tree, where they have been relaxing, after her father mistakenly mentions Trujillo's name in an unfavorable way. For Dede in 1994, this is "the moment she has fixed in her memory as zero," when the events that led to the deaths of her sisters began. Already there are spies who can report the family to Security for her father's negative comment. This quotation also foreshadows the known outcome of the family's history: earlier in the chapter, it has been established that Dede is, in fact, "the only one left to tell their story."

"And that's how I got free. I don't mean just going to sleepaway school on a train with a trunkful of new things. I mean in my head after I got to Inmaculada and met Sinita and saw what happened to Lina and realized that I'd just left a small cage to go into a bigger one, the size of our whole country."

Chapter 2, page 13

Minerva uses "free" to mean enlightened; at Inmaculada Concepcion, she realizes that the Trujillo she has believed in does not exist, and the seeds of a revolutionary are sown within her. This use of "free" fits with the idea of a liberating, "liberal" education. The cage metaphor recalls the theme of entrapment; because of the dictatorship in the Dominican Republic, none of its citizens is truly free except in the way Minerva describes here. Thoughts, at least, are free. Also, her home had been a cage of rules, while the country is a cage of violence and authoritarian rule.

"We've traveled almost the full length of the island and can report that every corner of it is wet, every river overflows its banks, every rain barrel is filled to the brim, every wall washed clean of writing no one knows how to read anyway."

Chapter 6, page 117

Minerva is driving back from the capital with her parents after Enrique Mirabal, now insane, is released from prison. The rainy weather is the physical incarnation of the metaphorical storm that began for the Mirabal family when Minerva slapped Trujillo at the Discovery Day dance: "And then the rain comes down hard, slapping sheets of it." It also represents Trujillo's power; the island is saturated in wetness as well as in the influence of the dictatorship. This quotation thus demonstrates the authoritarian theme that permeates the novel.

"Voz del pueblo, voz del cielo."

Chapter 9, page 199

This means, "Talk of the people, voice of God," and it is an old proverb. Dede says it to Minerva as she tries to convince her that the rumors that Trujillo wants her dead are not silly. She takes it to mean that popular opinion is always right, and in this case, it is. Minerva refuses to listen to her sister, calling the talk "silly rumors," but this is a mistake and she is killed. Mama also uses this proverb to warn Minerva about traveling to visit Puerto Plata. This phrase also is the title of the last section of the last chapter of the novel, told from Minerva's point of view. It is as if this section serves as proof that rumors are usually true, that the people have a certain wisdom, and that one should take warnings seriously.

"She took both my hands in hers as if we were getting ready to jump together into a deep spot in the lagoon of Ojo de Agua. 'Breathe slowly and deeply,' she intoned, 'slowly and deeply.'

"I pictured myself on a hot day falling, slowly and deeply, into those cold layers of water. I held on tight to my sister's hands, no longer afraid of anything but that she might let go."

Chapter 3, page 39

After Minerva tells Maria Teresa about the secret meetings she has been attending at Don Horacio's house, they have this experience together. It is the moment that Maria Teresa becomes part of the revolutionary movement, if only symbolically. By lying for her sister about their (not so) ill Tio Mon, she demonstrated her loyalty, but now she understands what she was lying about, and she is demonstrating her allegiance.

"What did I want? I didn't know anymore. Three years stuck in Ojo de Agua, and I was like that princess put to sleep in the fairy tale. I read and complained and argued with Dede, but all that time I was snoring away.

"When I met Lio, it was as if I woke up. The givens, all I'd been taught, fell away like so many covers when you sit up in bed."

Chapter 6, page 86

24   Quotes and Analysis

It is interesting here that Alvarez has Minerva use the metaphor of a princess in a fairy tale, since Minerva, of all the sisters, represents a reversal in the traditional role of women. Lio, the revolutionary, inspires her and changes the course of her life. Waking up is representative of realizing how she can become involved in the revolution and bring about change in her own life, by having something to dedicate herself to instead of "snoring away," as well as representing how she can bring about change for the Dominican Republic.

"And on the third day He rose again ..."

Chapter 10

Patria repeats this phrase as a mantra throughout Chapter 10. It is a reference to Jesus' rising from the dead on Easter, and it reflects the struggle Patria has felt throughout the novel to reconcile her heavenly self with her responsibilities on earth. She draws a connection between herself and Jesus; she is going through her own trials, waiting for her son, Nelson, to be released from prison. The theme of Trujillo trucking on Jesus' reputation is interlaced with her own connection to Jesus, for she prays to Trujillo every time she passes his portrait. She prays to him, "Take me instead, I'll be your sacrificial lamb."

Summary and Analysis of Part I - Chapter One: Dede, 1994 and circa 1943

It is March 1994, and Dede is arranging an interview with a "gringa dominica" to talk about her sisters. The only thing unusual about this interview is that it is taking place in March, not November, which is the anniversary of her sisters' death and when most interviewers come calling. She has given the woman directions to her home, and they plan to meet there that afternoon. As Dede tidies up the appearance of her garden, the reader learns that she became a successful insurance salesperson after her divorce ten years ago.

At three o'clock, she hears a car door slam as the interviewer arrives. Dede gives her a tour of the house where she and her sisters grew up. They stop in front of three pictures of the sisters when they were young, and Dede realizes that she misses her own young self more than she misses her sisters. Her picture is not there, and she explains to the woman, "I have this hallway just for the girls." The woman reveals that she knows hardly anything about the family when she asks where Dede comes in the birth order. This is a relief for Dede, since now she can spend the time talking about "the simple facts that give Dede the illusion that hers was just an ordinary family, too."

She describes her sisters in brief sound bites as if she is "pinning [them] down with a handful of adjectives." These brief descriptions provide a first, basic look at each of her sisters. When Dede asks the interviewer what she wants to know, the interviewer answers, "Tell me all of it." Then she comments on how "open and cheerful" Dede is, and she expresses wonder about how Dede manages to keep from letting "such a tragedy" take her under. Dede explains that she tells herself to focus on the happy years, and she plays over the happy memories in her head, like a movie.

Dede's mind "is already racing backwards, year by year, to the moment she has fixed in her memory as zero." Now it is circa 1943 on "a clear moonlit night before the future began." The whole family is out in the front yard under the anacahuita tree, relaxing and telling stories. Papa, Enrique Mirabal, is drinking rum and getting a bit drunk while the others drink guanabana juice. A campesino comes by, begging for calmante and tobacco; Papa gives them to him, as well as a few mints for his godchildren. When Dede teasingly scolds him for giving everything away, he predicts that she "is going to be the millionaire in the family."

Maria Teresa, age eight, asks about her own fortune, and her father tells her she will make "a lot of men's mouths water." When Patria asks him, "What of me?" Enrique enlists the help of his wife, Chea Mirabal, but she scolds him, reminding him that "fortunes are for those without faith." Minerva points out that their father is not doing anything wrong, since "Padre Ignacio condemns fortunes only if you believe a human being knows what only God can know." Maria Teresa joins in, defending Minerva, and mentions that she played with a Ouija board with Padre Ignacio and her cousins Berto and Raul. It predicted that she would become a lawyer, which is what Minerva actually wants to be.

Mama playfully comments that they don't need "skirts in the law," but Minerva jumps in and says that it's about time women had some say in how the country was run. Papa says, "You and Trujillo," and immediately the mood becomes tense as they realize he has mentioned Trujillo's name outdoors in the quiet night. Spies could be lurking anywhere, though there is not yet any suspicion about the Mirabal family. They all hurry inside.

Analysis

Unlike those of her sisters, Dede's chapters are narrated in third person. However, Alvarez uses the technique of rhetorical questions to imply that the reader is, at times, inside Dede's head, with access to what she is thinking or wondering. For instance, when Dede questions why the woman is coming to interview her in March, not in November like most interviewers, she thinks, "Doesn't she have seven more months of anonymity?" When the narrator explains that everyone wants to buy insurance from her because she is famous, she asks, "Can she help it?"

As Dede describes her sisters for the interviewer, she feels as if she is pinning them down "with a handful of adjectives." She is spouting out the usual descriptions that must be used to talk about them in biographies and articles, removed from who they really were. But during her interview with the woman, she can be transported back to the time when they were alive, remembering them as actual people rather than just as myths. That is also what Alvarez does with *In the Time of the Butterflies*, making the sisters into developed characters rather than just heroes.

In this first chapter, Enrique Mirabal is characterized as a drinker. Alvarez uses indirect characterization; Dede does not simply tell the interviewer that her father drank too much; rather, in her memory, she "hears the clink of the rum bottle against the rim of his glass." Similarly, as he attempts to tell their fortunes later, "Papa burps, slurring his words." Enrique also is characterized as generous when he gives the begging campesino medicine, cigars, and mints for his godchildren. Dede comments that she does not know how they continue being so well off when he gives everything away. Maria Teresa and Mama are characterized by their own words and by Dede's comments in hindsight.

Maria Teresa's admiration of Minerva is already apparent in this first chapter, as Dede remembers them talking of the future. She "defends her adored older sister," insisting that predicting fortunes is not a sin. She says, "I asked the talking board what I would be when I grew up, and it said a lawyer." She is imitating her older sister, since Minerva actually is hoping to go to law school.

When Mama scolds Papa for telling fortunes, Dede thinks, "Ay, Mama, ease up a little on those commandments. Work out the Christian math of how you give a little and you get it back a hundredfold." The violent imagery that permeates the entire novel is apparent already in the first chapter, as Enrique Mirabal jokes about how quickly he had four daughters: "Bang-bang-bang, their father likes to joke, aiming a finger pistol at each one, as if he were shooting them, not boasting about having sired them." The joke is about their births—with a bit of phallic imagery added in. The violent side of the imagery foreshadows their deaths.

The chapter also ends with foreshadowing as the family goes inside. Dede remembers, "A chill goes through her, for she feels it in her bones, the future is now beginning. By the time it is over, it will be the past, and she doesn't want to be the only one left to tell their story." The reader knows already that Dede *is* the only one left, and that she is telling the story to the interviewer. This is repetitive foreshadowing since it does not reveal any new information but shows the emotional power of the events in Dede's mind.

Summary and Analysis of Part I - Chapter Two: Minerva, 1938, 1941, 1944

Complications, 1938

Minerva relates that she and her sisters had to ask permission for everything, including being able to go away to school. Papa gave permission for Patria to go to Inmaculada Concepcion because she wanted to become a nun, so Minerva asks if she can go along. Dede volunteers to be the one to stay and help Enrique Mirabal with his store until January.

At school, Minerva meets Sinita Perozo during the greeting of the new pupils. They make friends when Minerva offers Sinita a shiny button. Sinita is a "charity student," but Minerva defends her against the girls who tease her, and Sor Milagros allows them to choose beds next to each other. Sor Milagros gives the girls a talk about "personal hygiene," explaining what to do when they begin to menstruate. She calls it their "complications." After Minerva explains more about menstruation to Sinita, Sinita tells her she has a secret.

A couple of weeks later, Sinita reveals the secret during the night while Minerva lies beside her in bed. Trujillo destroyed her family, killing her uncles, her father, and her brother. Minerva considers, for the first time, that Trujillo is not the saint he makes himself out to be, and she feels as if she is going to throw up. When she wakes up the next morning, she realizes that she has begun menstruating: "my complications had started."

¡Pobrecita!, 1941

Minerva and her friends, Sinita, Elsa Sanchez, and Lourdes, all look up to Lina Lovaton, who is beautiful and is a couple of years older than they are. One day while they are outside playing volleyball, Lina is summoned to meet Trujillo. He has seen her playing volleyball and has insisted upon meeting her. He begins to visit the school often to see her, bringing gifts for her and for the nuns. He even throws her a huge party for her seventeenth birthday. Lina says she has fallen in love with him. But after her birthday party, Lina doesn't return to the school. Minerva learns from her Papa that she was taken to live in a big house as one of Trujillo's girlfriends.

Unfortunately, Lina became pregnant, and Trujillo's wife went after her with a knife. Trujillo was forced to ship her off to Miami where she would be safe, living all alone. Minerva and Sinita talk about how sorry they feel for her. Although Sinita exclaims that Trujillo is a devil, Minerva thinks that he is just a man. She imagines that he feels remorse and has nightmares about what he has done.

The Performance, 1944

Celebrations for the centennial of the Dominican Republic have been going on since Independence Day on February 27. To show their loyalty to Trujillo, the Mirabal family members make the celebration of Patria's twentieth birthday into a patriotic affair. At school, the girls are issued new history textbooks that paint Trujillo as the country's savior—"it was pretty disgusting." A new wing has been added to their school building. It is called the Lina Lovaton Gymnasium. There is going to be a recitation contest with a centennial theme, and Minerva, Sinita, Elsa, and Lourdes decide to enter together.

Minerva and her friends win the recitation contest. They learn that they will be sent to the capital to perform for Trujillo on his birthday. Minerva does not want to go, but Sinita begs her to go, saying that their play is not about Trujillo but about "a time when we were free. It's like a hidden protest." They decide to do the skit dressed as boys.

They drive to the capital and wait in the palace anteroom. They are ushered into the hall, where Trujillo is sitting next to his son, Ramfis, whispering. The girls begin the skit and gain confidence as the performance goes on. At the point when Sinita is supposed to step forward and show off her bow and arrow, she breaks from the script and walks toward Trujillo's chair, taking aim at him. Ramfis jumps up, grabs her bow, and asks for her name. When she says it is Perozo, he realizes what family she is from, and he orders her to untie Minerva, saying, "Use your dog teeth, bitch!" Released, Minerva begins the chant, "¡Viva Trujillo!" On the way home, they are scolded by Sor Asuncion for their behavior.

Analysis

The dire situation of life in the Dominican Republic is portrayed symbolically when Minerva describes wanting to leave home. Minerva considers herself trapped at home, perceiving Inmaculada Concepcion as a kind of escape. She sees her own situation mirrored in that of the rabbits in their pens, but she realizes that she is nothing like a rabbit when the rabbit that she tries to let free refuses to leave the cage. As for her, however, "I'd just left a small cage to go into a bigger one, the size of our whole country."

The title of the section "Complications" refers to Minerva's becoming a woman physically, given that this is the euphemism Sor Milagros uses for menstruation. Growing up happens in many ways at once as one matures. Emotionally, the complications for Minerva involve learning about Trujillo's evil—on the night that she begins to menstruate. The two forms of growing up are linked with a simile. As Minerva listens to Sinita's story, "the aching in my belly was like wash being wrung so tightly, there wasn't a drop of water left in the clothes." Both kinds of complications are painful and gut-wrenching, leaving her feeling drained.

The section "¡Pobrecita!" tells the story of Lina Lovaton's tragic relationship with Trujillo. It begins with a country saying: "until the nail is hit, it doesn't believe in the hammer." This phrase about oblivious innocence expresses that Minerva does not realize the extent of the damage Trujillo can cause until one of her own classmates' lives is ruined because of him, right before her eyes. At the end of the section, when Minerva considers what has become of Lina Lovaton, a simile hearkens back to the country saying: "downstairs in the dark parlor, the clock was striking the hours like hammer blows." These sayings continue the violent imagery earlier in the novel.

More such violent imagery introduces Sinita's anecdote about Trujillo having all the men in her family killed. Although Minerva asks her to stop talking, "Sinita's story spilled out like blood from a cut." This image is a little melodramatic, but readers should remember the relative immaturity of the child's perspective. Similarly, in explaining that she, Sinita, Elsa, and Lourdes are inseparable friends, Minerva relates, "Sor Asuncion was always joking that when we graduated in a couple years, she was going to have to hack us apart with a knife."

Indeed, as narrator, Minerva often uses simile in descriptions, and often it is violent. When Ramfis jumps up to grab the bow from the approaching Sinita before she reaches his father Trujillo, he moves "quick as gunfire." Minerva also uses less violent imagery when conveying an emotion connected with the action. For instance, after Sinita tells Minerva that Trujillo had three of her uncles shot, she "took a deep breath as if she were going to blow out all her grandmother's birthday candles." Of course, a deep breath would be needed to blow out the many candles marking the age of an old woman. But her grandmother would also be the mother of the three uncles who were shot, so this simile points out the loss of family and hope—the blowing out of all the lights—in her family. Finally, taking a deep breath signifies the emotional gravity of the story she has been telling.

Summary and Analysis of Part I - Chapter Three: Maria Teresa, 1945 to 1946

Maria Teresa's narration is in diary form. She received the diary from Minerva for her First Communion. She finds it difficult to reflect. She reports that the girls at school steal the diary and make fun of her. Maria Teresa interprets her First Communion as meaning that now she *really* has a soul, and she asks Minerva what that even means. Maria Teresa also talks to the diary as if it is her friend. She also notes that she is "advanced" for her age, since she has three older sisters, and that she does not much like Inmaculada Concepcion.

In December, Maria Teresa records taking the train home for the holidays with Minerva. On the train, Minerva explains about menstruation and sex. A young man who has been following them, saying Minerva is "the most beautiful woman he'd ever seen," offers them cashews, and he comments on the drawing of a penis that Minerva has been showing to Maria Teresa.

At home, Patria has brought over her two children, Noris and Nelson, and is pregnant with a third. Maria Teresa makes "resolves" for the new year, including not scaring Nelson with scary stories. She goes shopping in Santiago with Mama and Minerva, who talks Mama into letting her buy a new swimsuit. Maria Teresa's cousins, Berto and Raul, come to visit with Tia Flor. Even at her young age, Maria Teresa thinks they are very "special-minded," especially Berto, who brought them roses.

On Three Kings Day, Minerva awkwardly mentions that they ought to celebrate Benefactor's Day at the cemetery. Maria Teresa does not understand what she means. On Benefactor's Day, Maria Teresa takes "these few minutes to wish El Jefe Happy Benefactor's Day with all my heart. I feel so lucky that we have him for a president."

Back at school in January, Maria Teresa feels homesick and lonely. In February, she is summoned to the principal's office to vouch for Minerva, who has been sneaking out of school. Minerva says it is to visit their sick uncle, Tio Mon, in La Vega, and Maria Teresa corroborates her lie. Later, she confronts her older sister, angry that she had to lie. Eventually, Minerva tells her that she, Elsa, Lourdes, and Sinita have been meeting secretly at Don Horacio's house, who is Elsa's grandfather. Knowing about Minerva's meetings, Maria Teresa begins to question Trujillo's benevolence. Tio Mon appears at the school unexpectedly, totally healthy, and Minerva must rush him away before he can give away that she was lying about his illness.

Minerva is now hanging around with the revolutionary Hilda, of whom Maria Teresa disapproves. Sor Asuncion says that Hilda has a bad attitude, and Maria Teresa thinks she is an orphan. In June, guards come looking for Hilda, who is hiding at Inmaculada Concepcion, pretending to be a student. In July, Minerva graduates and Patria miscarries, losing her son. She and Pedrito are staying at Mama's house until she recovers emotionally.

The diary ends with a rushed entry in which Maria Teresa explains that she must hand the book over to Minerva because it mentions Hilda. Hilda has been caught in the convent, and Minerva is burying everything that mentions her friend's name so as not to be implicated. Maria Teresa promises that "it won't be forever, my dear Little Book, I promise."

Analysis

Because Maria Teresa's chapters are narrated in diary form, her voice is affected by her age at the time. In this chapter, she is eleven and twelve years old. Although she does not understand some of what is going on, the reader can gather information from her reports. For instance, on Three Kings Day, when Minerva mentions that they should celebrate Benefactor's Day in a cemetery, Maria Teresa says, "I guess I do have a reflection. Why should we celebrate Benefactor's Day in the cemetery? I asked Minerva, but she said it was just a bad joke, forget she said so." The reader understands Minerva's meaning even if Maria Teresa does not.

Maria Teresa's devotion to and admiration of Minerva are apparent in this chapter, as she notes. Minerva is the one who gave her the diary, encouraging her to reflect as a way to "deepen one's soul." After her First Communion, when Maria Teresa asks Minerva what it means to *really* have a soul, "Minerva says a soul is like a deep longing in you that you can never fill up, but you try." She also demonstrates her commitment to Minerva by lying for her, corroborating the story that Tio Mon is ill and that this is why Minerva has been sneaking out of school.

In lying for Minerva, Maria Teresa indirectly becomes involved in her older sister's revolutionary activities. It is the beginning of their downfall, and this is expressed in a simile of jumping into water together: "She took both my hands in hers as if we were getting ready to jump together into a deep spot in the lagoon of Ojo de Agua ... I pictured myself on a hot day falling, slowly and deeply, into those cold layers of water. I held on tight to my sister's hands, no longer afraid of anything but that she might let go." Maria Teresa gradually learns more and more about the revolutionary activities, including the reason for Hilda's presence.

Maria Teresa's ideas about Trujillo change considerably during this chapter. On Benefactor's Day, she writes, "I feel so lucky that we have him as a president." But after Minerva tells her about the revolutionary meetings she is going to, Maria Teresa writes, "Everything looks just a little different ... Before, I always thought our president was like God, watching over everything I did." He might be always watching through his spies, but the constant judgments concern not human rights and human morality, as God's judgments might. Trujillo is judging adherence to his authoritarian regime. The comparison of Trujillo to divinity is a theme that runs throughout the novel. He is compared to God from the perspective of an innocent child, but as she matures she learns that this is not the right way to look at the nation's leader.

Finally, diction that evokes death appears throughout Maria Teresa's diary, setting a somber tone and in some ways foreshadowing the events to come. For example, when Minerva tells Maria Teresa about her revolutionary gatherings, Maria Teresa writes, "I swear my older sister will be the death of me!" When Minerva suggests that they should celebrate Benefactor's Day in the cemetery, "the room went silent as a tomb."

Summary and Analysis of Part I - Chapter Four: Patria, 1946

This chapter takes place in 1946, when Patria is 22 years old. She relates that she has always believed in God and suspected that she was to become a nun. At the age of 14 she went to school at Inmaculada Concepcion, and everyone suspected she would be going to the convent. When she is 15, Sor Asuncion has a talk with her and tells her to "listen deeply in case He is calling." But Patria is distracted by the coming storm she can see out the window.

For a while, Patria struggles against the sexual temptation she feels, trying to listen for God's call. On Holy Thursday, she volunteers to help Padre Ignacio by washing the feet of the parishioners, as is the tradition. One of the men whose feet she washes is Pedrito Gonzales, and she knows immediately that she wants to be with him, although they do not speak. He stands out to her because of his animalistic qualities, not just in the way that he appears, but also in that she feels a certain pity for him, a need to take care of him.

In May, Sor Asuncion asks her if she has heard her calling, and at last Patria confesses that she has heard it—but it is not that she should be a nun. Patria does not return to school; instead she helps Papa with the store. They plan the wedding for February 24, before her seventeenth birthday. She is tempted to make love to Pedrito before their wedding when he pours dirt into her hand and declares his simple love for her, but she resists.

She and Pedrito move to San Jose de Conuco fifteen minutes away. She gives birth to Nelson and Noris, then becomes pregnant again. She is worried about Minerva, who is speaking out against the government. In worrying about Minerva's loss of faith, she begins to struggle with her own faith. Patria does not describe having a miscarriage other than as it is connected to losing her faith: "I realized I was giving birth to something dead I had been carrying inside me." But after losing her baby, she wonders if she is being punished for giving up on her religious calling.

Patria and Pedrito move back into their family's home with the children in August. In nursing Pedrito's spirit back to health, Patria finds herself healing as well. One night, she follows him outside when he sneaks out of bed, and she witnesses him digging what looks like a little grave. Afraid that he has reburied their dead baby in unconsecrated ground, she enlists campesinos to dig up the grave in the cemetery and check, under the pretence that she has forgotten to include the baby's Virgencita medallion. But when she sees the baby "swarming with ants," "decomposing like any animal," she is horrified and feels herself losing her faith.

Chea Mirabal decides to take all her daughters on a pilgrimage to Higuey, where there have been sightings of the Virgencita. On the drive there, Chea speaks a bit too flippantly about her husband, and Patria begins to wonder why Mama wanted to go on the pilgrimage. Mama declares, "They're all scoundrels—Dominicans, Yanquis, every last man ... yes, your father, too." She will not elaborate, but Patria understands that her father must have been unfaithful. When they reach Higuey it is filled with pilgrims, so the women decide to stay with distant relations who live there. Patria shares a bed with Chea, and after they pray the rosary, Patria asks her mother, "What's wrong, Mama? ... Another woman?" Her mother confirms it.

The next morning they set out for the chapel, lying to their hosts and saying they are fasting so as not to bother them by taking their food. They wait in line to approach the altar among hordes of other pilgrims and beggars. As Maria Teresa begins to pray, Patria feels her faith coming back to life. She imagines that when she asks the Virgin, "Where are you?" She is answered with, "Here, Patria Mercedes, I'm here, all around you. I've already more than appeared."

Analysis

Here as the narrator, Patria describes herself with similes both of life and of entrapment. She describes the way that she believes in God and loves "everything that lives" as automatic or natural, "like a shoot inching its way towards the light." However, during the moment of her birth, instead of being born hands first as it looked like she might be, at the last minute she "lowered my arms the way you fold in a captive bird's wings so it doesn't hurt itself trying to fly."

Also, when Sor Asuncion summons Patria to talk about listening for her calling from God, the storm that Patria notices brewing outside is a metaphor for the complex emotional situation that calls her not to living with the purity of a nun but to fulfill a more earthly calling: "Entering that sombre study, I could see just outside the window the brilliant red flames lit in every tree, and beyond, some threatening thunderclouds." When Sor Asuncion tells her to pray to the Virgencita for guidance, she "saw the first zigzag of lightning, and heard, far off, the rumble of thunder." These are hints that she is not meant to become a nun. As Patria prays with Sor Asuncion, she remembers, "I tried hard but I could not keep my eyes from straying to the flame trees, their blossoms tumbling in the wind of the coming storm." In a sense she is of the "flesh" rather than of the "spirit."

Pedrito similarly is described in terms of the earth, since to a large degree he represents Patria's earthly calling as opposed to a heavenly one. When she looks at him while washing his feet, she notices, "A young man was staring down at me, his face alluring in the same animal way as his feet." She calls him "my earthly groom," as opposed to God, who would be her heavenly one. He is so tied to the earth (not just because of his feet) that when he describes his love for her, he says, "You are getting a man who adores you like he does this rich soil we're standing on," and he pours a handful of dirt into her palm.

Patria uses direct address as the narrator, almost always with an exclamation, as if she is trying desperately to convince the reader of something. For instance, after describing her temptation with Pedrito, she exclaims, "You'd think there was nothing else but the private debates of my flesh and spirit going on, the way I've left out the rest of my life. Don't believe it! Ask anyone around here who was the easiest, friendliest, simplest of the Mirabal girls, and they'd tell you, Patria Mercedes."

In addition, the theme of the role of women emerges for Patria in this chapter, as she worries about Minerva getting worked up about the government. She says to her little sister, "It's a dirty business, you're right. That's why we women shouldn't get involved." But Minerva argues, "women had to come out of the dark ages."

Also, Trujillo is again compared to God; here, specifically the comparison is to Jesus. In this chapter, while Patria lies beside Minerva in the hammock, they look at the pictures of Jesus and El Jefe, hung side by side. Minerva notes, "They're a pair, aren't they?" This inspires Patria to question why God would allow their country to suffer so much at the hands of Trujillo. When she looks up to challenge the picture of Jesus, "the two faces had merged!" This experience points out the God-like role that Trujillo plays in the minds of the people. He is omniscient because of his "disciples" or spies, learning what everyone in the country is doing, and to a large degree he controls what is said and done and what the country provides its people.

Summary and Analysis of Part II - Chapter Five: Dede, 1994 and 1948

Back in the present (1994), Dede considers how Fela, their longtime servant, thinks that she is possessed by the spirits of the dead Mirabal sisters. She had accidentally come across Fela's shrine to the girls one Friday in the shed behind the house. She had ordered Fela to move the shrine, but Minou scolded her for being intolerant. Minou often stops at the shrine, which is now down the street. She asks Dede where Lio Morales now lives, since Minerva has asked her to deliver a message to him—just to say hello, and to state how much she thinks of him.

When the interview woman presses on, asking Dede, "When did all the problems start?" Dede begins to speak about Lio Morales. She met him one "hot and humid afternoon" while she was organizing her father's shop with Minerva. They are finishing up before they head to Tio Pepe's to play volleyball with their friends. Dede knows that her cousin Jaimito, on whom she has started to have a crush (even though he once annoyed her), will be there. Mario, one of their distributors, arrives with Lio, and introduces him as his cousin. He knows Elsa Sanchez and Sinita Perozo from the university. When Dede mentions that they are committed to playing volleyball, Minerva invites Mario and Lio. Minerva gets their father's permission, and the girls go to Tio Pepe's with Mario and Lio.

A few weeks later, Lio is still joining them for volleyball. Jaimito suggests that the girls come to play. As they take off their shoes and begin to assign positions, Dede notices that Minerva and Lio are missing. She is unsure if it is actually an accident, but she hits the ball into the hedges, startling the hiding couple. Once Lio emerges from the hedges, Jaimito starts a fight with him, and the game ends in awkwardness.

Lio and Jaimito both begin to come to the Mirabal house more and more. When Maria Teresa accidentally reads aloud to Mama a newspaper article that reveals that Lio is "a communist, a subversive," Mama becomes upset that she has been letting him spend time at their home. But Minerva continues to see him on double dates with Jaimito and Dede. Still, Minerva refuses to admit that she is in love with Lio.

When Dede asks him how he wants to accomplish his revolutionary goals, Lio cannot give her the direct answer she wants. Dede becomes more and more nervous as Lio's name continues to appear in the newspapers, and she and Minerva lie about spending time with him. Then Lio announces that he'll be going into exile with some of his comrades.

One night, after a gathering of the Dominican party in San Francisco, Jaimito asks Minerva if Lio has invited her to go into exile with him, and she says that he has not. Jaimito tells them that the police were looking for Lio at his house and that he was taken down to the station for questioning. He told them that Lio had given him girlie magazines to get them off his back.

Minerva leaves, and Dede and Jaimito begin to kiss. Jaimito tells her there is something he wants her to see out back. They get into Papa's car, and he slips a ring on her finger, proposing. But they are surprised by Lio's cough from the backseat—he has been hiding there. Jaimito is furious that he would endanger the Mirabals, but Lio gives Dede a letter to deliver to Minerva. As Dede walks Jaimito to his car, she agrees to marry him.

Alone, Dede decides not to tell Minerva that Lio is hiding in the backseat of Papa's car. She goes into her bedroom and opens the letter Lio asked her to deliver to Minerva. In it, he invites her to go into exile with him. Dede decides that she will not expose her sister to that danger, so she burns the letter in the lamp.

Analysis

This chapter reveals the tense relationship between Dede and Minerva. Their personalities are at odds: Minerva is full of questions and mischief, while Dede is much more organized and chooses to smile and dismiss things without stirring up trouble. But it is Lio who brings out Dede's resentment toward her sister. Though she loves Jaimito, Dede is jealous of Lio's interest in Minerva. She sees them as a glamorous couple doing exciting things, while she and Jaimito are merely expected to end up together. She exposes them hiding in the bushes together and even burns the letter from Lio that was intended for her sister. Dede tells herself it is to protect Minerva, but her action is clearly also out of jealousy that her sister might get involved in such a daring adventure with Lio.

As the narrator, Dede uses exclamations often, characterizing herself as someone whose placid, smiling demeanor is interrupted by bursts of emotion. When she considers her task of being "the grande dame of the beautiful, terrible past" by relating her family's history to the woman interviewer, she exclaims, "But it is an impossible task, impossible!" In talking about her husband, she wonders, "But who could control Jaimito, only son of his doting mother, unquestioned boss of his five sisters!"

The metaphors of knotted string and captivation carry through this chapter, as Dede describes herself getting caught up in the twists and turns of life. When Lio teases her for going to play volleyball in a dress, "Suddenly, Dede feels foolish, caught in her frivolity as if she were a kitten knotted in yarn." As Dede reads articles in the paper about how people are getting arrested, "Dede's courage unraveled like a row of stitches not finished with a good, sturdy knot." Being sown up can be for protection or for captivation. She does not think Lio has a plan, and she becomes afraid to be involved with him.

The diction that Dede uses as narrator recounting the events of the past ties Minerva to death. After Maria Teresa reads to Chea Mirabal the article calling Lio a communist, Chea calls for Minerva, and "From her bedroom, the book she was reading still in hand, appeared the death of them all." Though the phrase "to be the death of" can be used lightly to mean someone is a handful, in this case, Minerva actually *is* the death of them all. When Lio announces that he is going to leave to go into exile with his comrades, "Minerva was deathly quiet." It is clear that Dede in some way blames Minerva for getting the family involved in politics and thus bringing about her own death and that of her sisters.

There is a hint of foreshadowing, too, at the end of the chapter, when Dede considers Jaimito's marriage proposal. She is not surprised by it because she has always seen it as inevitable that she would marry Jaimito. "There was no question - was there? - but that they would spend the rest of their lives together." Notably, the question that interrupts her thought is both in the young Dede's mind and in the memory of the older Dede in 1994, remembering how she felt and how she might have suspected that she and Jaimito would end up getting a divorce. Even when she thinks of Jaimito fondly, as he begins to propose, Dede from the present cannot help but check the enthusiasm she felt at the time: "Her spoiled, funny, fun-loving man. Oh, what a peck of trouble she was in for."

Summary and Analysis of Part II - Chapter Six: Minerva, 1949

What do you want, Minerva Mirabal? Summer

Minerva has been living at home for a few years, and rumors are starting about her being a lesbian. She also realizes that something is amiss between Mama and Papa. She is bored and jealous of Elsa and Sinita, who are studying in the capital. Out on drives, she begins to notice her father's Ford always parked in front of the same campesino family home. Four girls run out to the road, and she sees that they have Mirabal eyes. She realizes that Enrique Mirabal is their father and that they are her half-sisters.

Since Lio went away, Minerva has been having headaches and bad asthma. One afternoon she goes into her father's armoire and goes through the pockets of his clothes. She finds four letters addressed to her from Lio, and she reads them. He refers to his proposal that she leave the country with him, which of course Minerva knows nothing about. Furious, she drives the Jeep over to the campesino house where she knows she will find her father's Ford. He comes out and asks her what she wants, but she just speeds away. When Papa gets home that night, he leads Minerva outside into the garden, where he slaps her. But when he says she owes him respect, she tells him he has lost it.

Minerva has also found an invitation to one of Trujillo's private parties in her father's coat pocket; it specifically mentions that Minerva should attend. Mama is scared for Minerva's safety, so she insists that Pedrito, Patria, Dede, and Jaimito go along, too. Before the party, Papa sends the Ford to the shop, so Minerva drives him to his medical appointments in San Francisco. One day, he means to stop by the house he has bought for his ex-mistress and his other children after the appointment, and Minerva insists she be allowed to go along to meet them. She even meets Carmen, their mother, with whom Papa says he is no longer involved.

Discovery Day Dance, October 12

The family arrives at the party an hour late, having gotten lost. But Trujillo is late, too, as they learn from Manuel de Moya, his secretary of state. A table is reserved for the Mirabals, but Don Manuel tells Minerva she is going to sit with Trujillo. Finally El Jefe arrives, but he does not sit with Minerva; instead, she is entertained by Manuel de Moya. It is about to rain, but the tables are pushed back for dancing. When Don Manuel asks Minerva to dance, she says she has a headache and cannot. Patria brings her calmantes before Don Manuel returns with some for her as well. Finally, Minerva agrees to dance with him.

Soon, Trujillo becomes her partner. He flirts with her, and she tells him she wants to study in the capital to be a lawyer. But when he implies that he would like to "conquer" her, she says she is "not for conquest." He tells her the university is no place for women, mentioning the "communists and agitators," implying they have been caught. By mistake, Minerva blurts out, "Virgilio Morales?" She must backtrack and pretend she does not know Lio, and Trujillo believes her. When he pulls her inappropriately close, thrusting at her in a vulgar way, she slaps his face.

The rain begins immediately, and the party moves quickly inside. The Mirabals rush off, but Minerva forgets her purse. She and Patria cannot find it anywhere, and they assume that someone already brought it inside and that it will be mailed to them. But on the ride home, Minerva realizes that she has put the letters from Lio in the pocket of the lining.

Rainy Spell

The Mirabal family left the party before Trujillo did, which is against the law. Two guardias arrive at their house and say that Governor de la Maza wants to see Enrique Mirabal and Minerva immediately, but Mama says, "If she goes, I go." At the governor's palace, Papa is sent to the capital for questioning. He whispers to Minerva that she is to take money to the illegitimate family in San Francisco every two weeks until he is back. Minerva does so, but she cannot find the house in the rain. She sees Margarita, the oldest daughter, and asks her to lead her to her mother's house. Once there, Minerva gives Carmen the money and asks if she can enroll the daughters in school.

Minerva and Chea return to the capital to petition for Papa's release. They get a room at a hotel. At the Office of Missing Persons, Minerva meets a man who has named all his sons Pablo Antonio so that if one of them is captured, he can swear he is not the son they are looking for. But the man's case takes so long that there is not time to hear the Mirabals'.

The next morning they are woken at the hotel and taken to the National Police Headquarters for questioning, where Minerva is interrogated about Lio by General Federico Fiallo and Don Anselmo Paulino. She admits that she lied to El Jefe about not knowing Lio, but she says it was because she was afraid of displeasing him. She says she is no longer in communication with Lio. Manuel de Moya enters and suggests that "a private conference with El Jefe would be the quickest, most effective way to end all this nonsense." He means, of course, that Minerva should sleep with Trujillo, but she insists that her father and mother come along to the meeting.

Three weeks later, they see Trujillo. Papa has just been released, but he has gone mad due to his imprisonment. In Trujillo's office, it is revealed that Tio Chiche, one of Trujillo's friends, is related to Chea Mirabal. He is a gambler and Mama doesn't like him very much, but she jumps on this connection in order to appeal to Trujillo. Minerva notices a set of dice on Trujillo's desk, and she realizes that they are loaded. She makes a bet with him: they will roll the dice, and if she wins, she can go to law school, but if he wins, he gets to sleep with her. Minerva knows to use the heavier set of dice, and of course she wins, to Trujillo's annoyance. Minerva, Chea, and Enrique Mirabal drive home in the rain.

Analysis

As Minerva asks herself what she wants, she uses the conceit of "that princess put to sleep in the fairy tale." It is Lio who woke her up when she met him: "The givens, all I'd been taught, fell away like so many covers when you sit up in bed." This conceit is ironic, since Minerva is anything but the stereotypical woman of a fairy tale, waiting for a man to come and wake her up so her life can begin. In actuality, Minerva speaks out for women's rights and takes matters into her own hands.

Imagery of woven thread appears again in this chapter, as Minerva struggles with decisions about where her life should go: "Back and forth my mind went, weaving a yes by night and unraveling it by day to a no." The dilemma is whether she loves Lio; she cannot decide. The decision is made for her when he decides to seek asylum. The imagery appears again when Mama clings to her connection of Tio Chiche (a friend of Trujillo's) and Papa in his madness points out that "Chiche cheats too much. I won't play with him." As a result, "Mama's eyes are boring a hole in Papa. Our one lifeline in this stormy sea and Papa is cutting the rope she's been playing out."

Violent diction appears once again in this chapter, as it has throughout the novel. As Enrique Mirabal leads Minerva down the driveway into the garden, "The moon was a thin, bright machete cutting its way through patches of clouds." This metaphor is continued when Minerva describes its light as "sharp," and it foreshadows the slap she is about to receive from her father.

The theme of Trujillo being conflated with God comes out in the paper fans that the girls received at the party they went to, thrown by Trujillo. The fans had the Virgencita on one side and Trujillo on the other. The combination bothers Minerva: "Sometimes it was El Jefe's probing eyes, sometimes it was the Virgin's pretty face I couldn't stand to look at."

The events of the party are mirrored by the weather's progression to a rain storm. When they arrive at the party, "there is a strong breeze, announcing rain." When Minerva mentions Lio's name, "suspicion clouds the gaze" of Trujillo's face, and when she refuses to dance with Manuel de Moya initially, "a cloud of annoyance crosses his face." When Minerva slaps Trujillo, it is like the clap of thunder that begins the storm: "and then the rain comes down hard, slapping sheets of it." In the midst of the storm, her family is the ship that steers her to safety: "Dede and Patria are turning in all directions like lookouts on the mast of a ship." Completing the conceit, Minerva steals a little decorative ship as a souvenir for Maria Teresa, who was too young to attend the party. As they escape in the rain, it looks as though the ship is being steered safely through the storm.

But there are two problems. Once Minerva realizes she has left the letters from Lio in the forgotten purse, all hope is lost. She feels something hard against her leg and reaches down to discover "the little caravel sunk in the folds of my damp dress." And the family has committed a crime by leaving the party before Trujillo. If Trujillo is the captain of a doomed autocratic ship, protocol states that the captain is to leave last; but at this point the regime is still strong and can arbitrarily declare that the nation's captain must be allowed to leave first. The resistance still has a long way to go.

Summary and Analysis of Part II - Chapter Seven: Maria Teresa, 1953 to 1958

Maria Teresa writes this chapter in her new journal, another gift from Minerva. Enrique Mirabal has passed away, and Maria Teresa is outraged that Carmen and her four daughters attended the funeral. Maria Teresa is struggling with her father's death. She had a troubling dream in which she found her wedding dress inside her father's coffin. She has the same dream again in February, but this time Manolo, Minerva's husband-to-be, is in the coffin. In October, while she is a student at the university, she again has the dream, but now it is Armando Grullon, one of Minerva's friends, in the coffin.

She has also developed crushes on both her cousins, Raul and Berto, and she asks Fela to help her determine which of the brothers she will marry. She kisses Berto on the lips on January 1 but is confronted about it by Raul on January 8. These events cause her to become fed up with both of them. Meanwhile, Tio Chiche has suggested that Mama write a letter to Trujillo affirming their loyalty to his regime. Maria Teresa is helping her write it, just as she helped Minerva with her speech at the Salcedo Civic Hall in which she praised Trujillo (earning permission to go to law school). But Fela has helped her put a curse on the letter.

Minerva has fallen in love with a man at law school named Manolo, but he is engaged to someone else. She comes to visit in January, demonstrably in a revolutionary mindset, reciting Fidel Castro's words that she has heard on illegal radio stations. On Valentine's Day, she visits again, this time bringing Manolo along. Maria Teresa has cooked dinner and is completely taken with Manolo. By March, however, she becomes suspicious since he met Minerva while he was engaged to someone else.

Maria Teresa has arranged to live with Dede and Jaimito and their sons, Jaime Enrique and Jaime Rafael, in San Francisco during the week, and come home to Mama's house on the weekends. Unfortunately, their ice cream business is failing, and soon they decide to move back to Mama's house and help run Papa's store.

On July 3, Maria Teresa graduates. Tia Flor bakes a cake for the party. Tia Flor also confronts her and says that she needs to choose between her two sons, Raul and Berto. Maria Teresa responds that she wants neither one. Meanwhile, the family's yardboy, Prieto, has betrayed them by reporting to Security everything they have done. They cannot fire him, however, since it would look suspicious.

In September, Maria Teresa goes to join Minerva at the university in the capital, and they are roommates. While Minerva encourages Maria Teresa to stick with law, the younger sister eventually decides to switch to Philosophy and Letters. She meets one of Minerva's and Manolo's friends, Armando Grullon, who tries to kiss her.

Now it is 1955, and Minerva is getting married in the rain. She moves in with Manolo, and by December 11 she is pregnant. By April 1956, Maria Teresa has started using her diary as an "all-purpose supply book." She is attempting to write a speech to give as Miss University, and Minerva is advising her how much and when to mention Trujillo. Minerva has given birth to Minou and is helping her younger sister write the speech.

Now it is July 1957, and Maria Teresa writes that Minerva is moving to Monte Cristi with Manolo after graduation. Trujillo, however, plays a terrible trick on Minerva by not actually granting her a license to *practice* law; her diploma is useless. Maria Teresa helps Minerva set up her new home in Monte Cristi, and it comes out that Manolo is cheating on Minerva with another woman. By August, though, the couple is "on the mend," and Minerva credits Maria Teresa with bringing them back together.

In her entry of September 28, 1957, Maria Teresa reports that she accidentally intercepted a delivery of guns from Leandro (codename Palomino) to the house. Manolo and Minerva explain about the national underground that's forming, and Maria Teresa joins them. Maria Teresa begins to fall in love with Leandro. Maria Teresa becomes a hub of a revolutionary cell, living with Sonia and storing deliveries in the "munitions room." While Sonia is away in La Romana, Leandro comes over and says that he is going to stay with Maria Teresa to protect her. Maria Teresa ends up marrying Leandro on Valentine's Day, 1958.

Analysis

Because of the diary style of Maria Teresa's narration, often the reader must figure out what is being referred to because of the lack of specifics. For example, in the December 15 entry, Maria Teresa writes, "I can't believe she came to the funeral mass with her girls" without saying who "she" is. It is as if she is in such an upset state of mind that she doesn't bother to explain herself (after all, it is a diary and Maria Teresa knows who she is talking about). The reader infers that she must be referring to Carmen.

In one sense, Maria Teresa's story is told via Minerva, since both diaries were gifts from her older sister. Yet, in this chapter the reader learns about many important events in Minerva's life through Maria Teresa's diary entries. For instance, we learn in Maria Teresa's report about the speech at Salcedo Civic Hall that Minerva has gained permission to attend law school. We also learn about Minerva's marriage to Manolo, the birth of Minou, and Trujillo's denial of her license to practice law upon graduation from law school. It is important to remember that we are learning about the events primarily from one point of view. The personal, family matters are related in the diary, while the political matters are often underground enough not to make it into the diary, generally because Maria Teresa does not know much of what is going on. By late 1957, however, the personal and political spheres are merging more quickly for her again.

As a narrator, Maria Teresa uses the technique of rhetorical questions, but they are influenced by the brooding nature of her diary entries. On December 31, 1953, as she looks out at the stars, she asks, "What does it all mean, anyway?" When Leandro spends the night on December 1, 1957, she writes, "Guess whose name was in my right shoe all day?" referring to the love spell Fela taught her years ago.

Another characteristic of Maria Teresa's narrative voice is the use of exclamations. After she kisses Berto, she exclaims, "Oh horror! Oh shamelessness! Oh disgust!" In July, when she eats two pieces of the cake Tia Flor cooked for her graduation party, she writes, "My hips, my hips!" This technique characterizes her as an emotional, dramatic woman. Even in a serious situation, such as when Minerva sobs before telling Maria Teresa that Manolo is cheating on her, Maria Teresa writes, "My brave Minerva!"

Death seems to lurk throughout the chapter. Of course, Enrique Mirabal has actually died, and Maria Teresa's recurring dream revolves around a coffin. But she also uses language that calls death to mind. The chapter opens with her statement, "I feel like dying myself!" When she comes back to her diary on July 3, she writes, "Diary, I know you have probably thought me dead all these months."

Summary and Analysis of Part II - Chapter Eight: Patria, 1959

Patria's children, Nelson and Noris, have grown up, and they all live in Pedrito's great-grandfather's house. Eighteen years after getting married, she has spent New Year's Eve at Mama's new house in Conuco, and she has fallen asleep at her own house. But she is woken up by Minerva, Manolo, Leandro, and Nelson, who report that Fidel Castro and Ernesto "Che" Guevara have ousted Batista in Cuba. That night, Raul Ernesto, Patria's next son, is conceived.

Patria is afraid for her sisters and for her son Nelson, who is "always tagging along behind his Tio Manolo and his new Tio Leandro, men of the world who had gone to the university and who impressed him more than his country father." She sends him to Santo Tomas de Aquino, a seminary in the capital, with the help of Padre de Jesus Lopez. When Nelson begins to talk about joining the liberators, Patria goes to Padre de Jesus Lopez for help, but he tells her he, too, is lost, and cannot show her the way.

Minerva and Maria Teresa both have had babies, Manolito and Jacqueline, respectively. Minerva asks Patria to take care of Manolito, explaining that she is going to "be on the road a lot." But she and Manolo visit from Monte Cristi every week; they meet on Patria's and Pedrito's land with many other revolutionaries. But this gives Nelson the chance to get involved when he is home from school. He reports back to her that the revolutionaries are expecting an invasion by the liberators from Cuba.

Though she is pregnant with Raul Ernesto, Patria decides to go on a retreat with Padre de Jesus and the Salcedo group to Constanza. They are the Christian Cultural Group, led by four priests including Padre de Jesus and Brother Daniel. Trujillo has heard rumors of the pending invasion and has declared a state of emergency, but the retreat goes to Constanza anyway. They stay in a retreat house that resembles a nunnery, and Patria feels peaceful.

On June 14, while they listen to Brother Daniel speak about the Assumption, the mountainside is bombed. The first wave of the liberating invasion is the target, and as Patria watches, one of them (who is about Noris's age) is gunned down. The Christian Cultural Group comes back down the mountain, and Patria's family meets her on the road coming into town. In the newspaper, they read that 49 men and boys died in the attack. They read six days later that the second wave of the invasion force was intercepted and also defeated.

At the next meeting of the Christian Cultural Group, the mood has changed considerably: Padre de Jesus speaks like a revolutionary, and they change their name to Accion Clero-Cultural, or ACC. Their mission is to organize a powerful national underground. Patria volunteers Pedrito, Nelson, Minerva, Manolo, Maria Teresa, and Leandro for the organization. However, Pedrito becomes upset that the revolutionaries are meeting in their backyard, since a new law has been passed that will allow the government to confiscate the land of anyone found to be harboring any enemies of the regime. Patria is able to sway him when she reveals that their son Nelson is involved, too.

The Fourteenth of June Movement is founded then, in Patria and Pedrito's home. There are about forty people, with Manolo as president. They make bombs, called "nipples," and hide weapons. Patria sends Noris to Chea Mirabal's house, and they use her bedroom as an ammunitions room.

Analysis

As narrator, Patria uses similes and personification that connect her to both heaven and earth. When Padre de Jesus tells her he cannot help her because he, too, is lost, she says, "I was shaking like when a breeze blows through the sacristy and the votive candles flicker." She is in the place of the prayerful candles, being shaken by nature. When she is overwhelmed by the beauty of Constanza, she personifies the land and nature more generally as if it is tied to God: "Purple mountains reaching towards angelfeather clouds; a falcon soaring in a calm blue sky; God combing His sunshine fingers through green pastures straight out of the Psalms."

Pedrito also ties Patria to the Earth. This is evident in the language she uses to express not being worried about him like she worries about her sisters: "Pedrito didn't worry me. I knew he would always have one hand in the soil and the other somewhere on me."

Patria uses a style of narration that involves direct address and exclamations, characterizing herself as deliberate but also at times as emotional as her younger sister Maria Teresa. For example, when Nelson sees an excited look on her face after he tells her about the invasion, she says, "But you know why that look was there? I'll tell you." Similarly, when she explains why Noris does not want to go along with her to the retreat, she says, "I certainly couldn't talk her into a retreat with 'old ladies' and a bunch of bad-breath priests. (Lord forgive her!)."

When Noris meets her after the mountainside is bombed, Patria notices "a change in her, as if her soul had at last matured and began *its* cycles." This metaphor comparing the soul maturing to a menstrual cycle hearkens back to Chapter 2, in which Minerva begins her "complications" both physically and emotionally as she realizes the country is in danger, and the power and evil of Trujillo. It also is reminiscent of Maria Teresa, who in her diary entries as a young girl yearned to discover her soul.

Patria also struggles to reconcile her commitment to God with her desire to protect her family and defend her country. Symbolically, she and Maria Teresa make a list of the weapons they've assembled "in the pretty script we'd been taught by the nuns for writing out Bible passages." Even when the retreat house is bombed, she describes it spiritually: "His Kingdom was coming down upon the very roof of that retreat house." As they ride back down the mountain after the retreat, she says, "I tried looking up at our Father, but I couldn't see His Face for the dark smoke hiding the tops of those mountains."

This chapter also keeps the reader informed about the larger history. We learn about the role of Cuba and its revolutionaries. We also learn about the events of June 14 and the origins, filtered through the narrator, of the Movimiento 14 de Junio.

Summary and Analysis of Part III - Chapter Nine: Dede, 1994 and 1960

In the afternoon in 1994, it is getting late. Dede says goodbye to the interview woman just as Minou arrives. She says that she was at Fela's and that Fela reported the sisters "must finally be at rest," since they won't come to possess her. Dede explains that they have been there with her all afternoon. Minou asks Dede, "I mean, you all were so close, why didn't you go along with them?" and Dede is once again transported into the past.

One Sunday afternoon while Jaimito is in San Francisco with all three of their sons, Minerva, Patria, and Maria Teresa pay Dede a surprise visit. She has become solitary and feels as if Jaimito has become a "bossy, old-fashioned macho" who fails to notice her unhappiness. In the fall, Patria asked if she could bury some boxes in the cacao fields, but Jaimito refused, and Dede has been avoiding her sisters ever since. Now, they report that "something big" is about to happen in less than three weeks, and Maria Teresa asks her to join their cell.

When Dede asks if Jaimito is also invited, Minerva compares him to Enrique Mirabal, saying it is scared men like them who have kept Trujillo in power so long. They tell her not to decide if she wants to join them right at that moment, but to come to Patria's house on Sunday if she wants to. Dede silently decides to leave Jaimito the next Sunday and attend the meeting with her sisters. She has never really gotten over her unspoken love for Lio—secretly one night she listened to him on the radio.

As she plans her escape, Dede begins to worry about leaving her sons. On Friday, she asks Don Bernardo if she can accompany him to Salcedo so she can go to church and speak with Padre de Jesus about her fears. But Jaimito is suspicious, as well as furious that she is disobeying his wish that she not go. Nobody is at the rectory when she gets dropped off, so Dede spends the morning checking back every half hour and wandering around the shops. Finally she sees a truck pull up with Padre de Jesus in it, but recognizes the pine boxes in it because they look like those that Patria kept at her house. Realizing that Padre de Jesus is "one of them," and afraid that he will encourage her to join the revolutionaries, Dede flees.

Back at the house, Tinita tells her that Jaimito has gone to his mother's, Dona Leila's, home with the boys. Dede panics and goes to Chea Mirabal's home; Minerva, Maria Teresa, and their husbands are there as well. Manolo and Minerva drive Dede to her mother-in-law's house in San Francisco, where they find Jaimito and his sons. Sensing the tension in their marriage, Manolo suggests that Jaimito and Dede "take a honeymoon somewhere nice." Thus, that weekend, the time that she had meant to leave her husband, becomes a boring vacation for them both.

The next week, Leandro is arrested. At Mama's house, Maria Teresa tells Dede that the SIM had broken into their apartment and ransacked it, taking Leandro away. Patria arrives, a complete wreck. Pedrito and Nelson have also been arrested, and their home has been torn apart and burned to the ground. When Dede gets in touch with Minerva, she repots that Manolo was arrested the night before, too. A few days later, Minerva confesses to Dede that she has been diagnosed with tuberculosis and needs money to pay for medications. But before Dede can bring them, Minerva is also taken to prison.

Dede and Jaimito are able to rebuild some strength in their marriage in their effort to save her sisters. They drive over to Mama's house to tell her that Minerva has been taken away, but when they get there, Captain Pena is there to bring Maria Teresa to jail, too. In Mama's bedroom, Dede, Jaimito, Patria, Noris, and Chea pray before dissolving into tears. That night as she lies in bed, Dede is tempted to run away, but she convinces herself that she cannot. She plays the game Minerva taught her when they were young, the one in which she concentrates on a happy memory.

The narrator corrects Dede's memory, clarifying that she did not learn the happy memory game until Minerva taught it to her, after she was released from prison and was living at Mama's. Dede visits every day and argues with Minerva to stay home, since rumors are abuzz that Trujillo wants her killed. But when Dede cries, telling her sister she is going crazy worrying about her, Minerva teaches her the happy memory exercise as a way to comfort herself.

Analysis

Speaking to the interview woman, Dede addresses the theme of the role of women: "'Back in those days, we women followed our husbands.' Such a silly excuse. After all, look at Minerva. 'Let's put it this way,' Dede adds. '*I* followed my husband. *I* didn't get involved.'" She is aware that she is using it as an excuse for not supporting her sisters, something for which she still feels guilty.

As her three sisters come down the path, Dede uses a simile that hearkens back to the conceit of life as a thread, an image that has been running through the novel: "It was as if the three fates were approaching, their scissors poised to snip the knot that was keeping Dede's life from falling apart." This sense of dread is also foreshadowing the future, in particular the untimely deaths that will befall all three. After Minerva and Maria Teresa are taken away to jail in the capital, "Dede fought down the sob that twisted like a rope in her gut. She felt that if she let go, the whole inside of her would fall apart." It is as if the rope of sorrow is holding her together.

Violent imagery permeates this chapter as well, drawing attention to the tension that hangs in the air for the Mirabal family. When she greets her sisters after avoiding them for weeks, Dede smiles—"Miss Sonrisa, *armed* with smiles." While her sisters are arming themselves with weapons, she pretends that she is happy. As she scans her garden, the new bed where she has been working "was disturbing to see—among the established plantings—the raw brown earth like a wound in the ground."

As a narrator, Dede's use of exclamation in this chapter reflects her exasperation with her sisters as well as her growing sense of panic. When Maria Teresa asks her to join their revolutionary cell, Dede says it is "As if they were inviting her to join a goddamn volleyball team!" This simile is meaningful since it was the volleyball game of their youth that first drew a line in the sand between Dede and Jaimito and Minerva and Lio, the revolutionaries. When Minerva asks if Dede could take some money out of her share of the house and lands in the future, so as not to have to borrow anything, Dede exclaims, "Too proud to just plain ask for help!"

Patria's struggle to reconcile heaven and earth comes to a climax in this chapter as she breaks down on Mama's front lawn. She tears up the grass from the ground around her, screaming. Dede gets down on her knees and puts the ground back in place, and "in a soothing voice, she reminded her sister of the faith that had always sustained her." Dede leads Patria in reciting the Credo, helping her find refuge in heaven when Pedrito, who connects her to earth, has been taken from her.

The theme of courage is apparent at the end of this chapter, when Dede lies in bed tempted to "just let go," meaning to stop trying to maintain her sanity. But she talks herself out of it, thinking, "Courage! It was the first time she had used that word to herself and understood exactly what it meant." For Dede, it means staying strong for her family and not selfishly running away. Indeed, courage is much needed at a time when the authorities are cracking down quite successfully on her family. This is a high point of tension for her and for the narrative.

Summary and Analysis of Part III - Chapter Ten: Patria, January to March 1960

For three months, Patria (along with the rest of the family) suffers without her son, husband, or Minerva. She is staying at Chea Mirabal's new home together with Maria Teresa, Dede, and their children. But after three days, the SIM comes to take Maria Teresa, too. Soon after she is taken, Captain Pena arrives, scaring the children. He tells her that the SIM made her husband an offer: he would get his freedom and farm back if he divorced "his Mirabal wife," but Pedrito refused.

At church the next Sunday, Padre Gabriel, the replacement after Padre de Jesus was arrested, gives a revolutionary sermon. The family spends the rest of the day in Salcedo attending masses. The church as an institution has "thrown in its lot with the people," and the SIM is noticing. The next Sunday, prostitutes attend mass and disrupt it; the next week, the contents of latrines are dumped in the confessional before Sunday morning.

One morning, Margarita, Carmen's daughter, comes to the house to deliver a note from Maria Teresa. She says that her mother's cousin works in La Victoria, the prison where the girls are being held. That night, Dede, Patria, and Chea stay up preparing a package to smuggle into the prison, with a note asking for any news of the men and Nelson. Patria delivers it to Margarita at the pharmacy where she works. After Mama goes to bed, Dede confesses to Patria that although her marriage seems to be bearable right now, Jaimito "would have been happier with someone else."

Now, the family is very aware of the spies who constantly lurk around their house. When they trample Mama's flower beds, she replaces the flowers with thorn bushes to trip them up so that they cannot get too close to the house. The newspaper reports that eight prisoners have been pardoned, which gives Patria hope; however, Captain Pena has taken over Patria and Pedrito's land.

Patria goes to Don Bernardo's house and asks for a ride to Santiago to Captain Pena's office. While she pleads with him to intercede on behalf of her family in jail, she prays for him all the while, hoping to defeat him with prayer. Meanwhile, the Catholic Church is being attacked by the government for its revolutionary pastorals. Patria continues to pray to Trujillo for the release of her family, and the correspondence via Margarita continues with the girls in jail.

Captain Pena comes to Chea Mirabal's house, but Mama refuses to see him, so it is Patria who must receive him. He brings visiting passes and reports that Nelson might be released with the next round of pardons. But Minerva and Maria Teresa have refused their own pardons. When Pena asks Patria how they should celebrate when Nelson returns home, she invites him over for a *sancocho*. That night, Patria confesses to her mother that she has "made an indiscreet promise," offering the Lord her own self in exchange for Nelson.

On the next Tuesday, they drive to the capital to pick up Nelson. They have their "most respectable relations," Tio Chiche and his son Blanco, escort them as a show of strength. Patria is worried that El Jefe will play a cruel trick and decide not to release Nelson, and she also worries for the sake of Noris, who has become beautiful and might be to Trujillo's liking. When he is released to Patria, she "cried out and dropped to my knees." Journalists record the release of all the pardoned prisoners, and it is reported in the newspaper.

Analysis

The theme of Trujillo being juxtaposed with Jesus is also prominent for Patria throughout this chapter. In Mama's old house, portraits of Jesus and Trujillo hung side by side, and now Patria says, "Maybe because I was used to the Good Shepherd and Trujillo side by side in the old house, I caught myself praying a little greeting as I walked by." She wants her family back from him, and "prayer was the only way I knew to ask." But when Patria arrives at the capital for the release of Nelson, she feels no kinship toward him—quite the opposite: "The more I tried to concentrate on the good side of him, the more I saw a vain, greedy, unredeemed creature. Maybe the evil one had become flesh like Jesus!"

Throughout this chapter, Patria also links herself to Jesus in her suffering. The very first line is, "I don't know how it happened that my cross became bearable," following Jesus' injunction to take up the cross and follow his ways. Also, as Jesus carried a cross and wore a crown of thorns in part as political torture, Patria says, "My crown of thorns was woven of thoughts of my boy." In addition, though she repeats as a mantra, 'And on the third day He rose again," after three days at her mother's house, "instead of a resurrection, I got another crucifixion," when the SIM comes to take Maria Teresa away. When she prays to Trujillo for the safe return of her family, she thinks, "Take me instead, I'll be your sacrificial lamb." In Christian tradition, Jesus is the lamb of God in that he dies to take away the sins of the world, suffering so that humans might live. Patria wishes to offer herself up as Jesus did in the Christian faith, for her family.

In contrast, Captain Pena is figured as the devil. When Don Bernardo drives Patria to his office, she says, "It wouldn't have been exaggerating to say that Patria Mercedes had been struck dumb in the devil's den." When it strikes her that he, too, is weak, she realizes: "This devil might seem powerful, but finally I had a power stronger than his." That power is prayer, and she prays for him: "Soften his devil's heart, oh Lord." When he comes to the house with visiting passes, Mama won't see him because "The truth was the devil was the devil even in a halo. But I knew it was more complicated than that. He was both, angel and devil, like the rest of us."

The violent imagery that has permeated all the sisters' narrations persists in this chapter. When Captain Pena tells Patria the offer that the SIM made Pedrito, she says, "I could feel my heart like a hand making a fist in my chest." When she speaks to him, "my voice threw sparks."

As the narrator, Patria uses the technique of rhetorical questions, in a sense implying dialogue, but also expressing the unspoken points that the characters all understand. For instance, when Mama and Dede see the black towel they sent Maria Teresa airing out the window of La Victoria, they know it means that it is her window: "And who else would have a black towel in prison?" When they hear the news that Captain Pena has taken over Patria and Pedrito's land, Mama stops herself from saying, "The truth is ..." because, "Why give out the valuable truth to a hidden microphone?"

Like that of her sisters, Patria's narrative voice is interrupted by exclamations that demonstrate her passion. When nothing happens in response to her prayers to Trujillo, she thinks, "Either Pena had forgotten or—God forbid!—something terrible" had met Nelson. When Pena comes to Mama's new house complaining that none of his neighbors will lend a hand to help him at the farm he has stolen from Patria and Pedrito, she thinks, "(What could he expect? That whole area was full of Gonzalez!)."

Summary and Analysis of Part III - Chapter Eleven: Maria Teresa, March to August 1960

Maria Teresa is writing in a notebook smuggled in to her by Santiclo, Carmen's cousin, who is one of the guards at La Victoria. She, Minerva, and the rest of the "woman politicals" are locked in a cell with sixteen "nonpoliticals," some of whom are serving time for dangerous crimes. Minerva and another revolutionary leader, Sina, hold classes and discussions in the southeast corner. One of the nonpolitical prisoners, Dinorah, has a terrible attitude about the "rich women." But Maria Teresa befriends one of the other women, Magdalena, who also has a little daughter.

Periodically, they are taken for questioning and put through humiliating ordeals. But they keep in touch with the men in the adjacent cell by using a knocking code. In the "little school" that Minerva holds every day, they rehearse three cardinal rules: "Never believe them. Never fear them. Never ask them anything." Maria Teresa struggles with panic and tries to plan a daily schedule to "ward off the panic that sometimes comes over me." She is especially upset that Minerva convinced her to refuse to be released with some of the other politicals out of principle.

On April 2, Maria Teresa writes about the Crucifix Plot. As a demonstration of solidarity, the prisoners have been wearing crucifixes and singing. Because of the suspicion surrounding the Catholic Church, Trujillo ordered that the crucifixes be taken away. When Minerva resisted, fighting with the guards, she was put in solitary. As she is being led there, the prisoners call out, "¡Viva la Mariposa!"

On April 7, Patria, Mama, and Pedrito visit Maria Teresa and tell her that Nelson is free and Leandro is being held in La 40. Though this news is uplifting for her, Maria Teresa is still feeling very depressed. She has missed three periods and is worried that she is pregnant; moreover, the guards might make her carry her baby to term and then "give it to some childless general's wife like the story Magdalena told me. That *would* kill me."

But a few days later, on April 11, Maria Teresa reports, "I've either bled a baby or had a period. And no one had to do a thing about it after the SIM got to me." The reader does not find out until the end of the chapter that Maria Teresa was taken to La 40 and whipped in front of Leandro, to try to convince him to do a job for Trujillo, though it is not described what the job is. It worked; Leandro cried out, "I'll do it! I'll do it!"

Magdalena and Balbina, a deaf prisoner, nurse Maria Teresa back to health. Minerva returns from solitary, but Maria Teresa cannot bring herself to tell her sister the details of what happened to her in La 40; Magdalena is the only one she tells. At Minerva's urging, she writes the incident down. On Monday, May 23, Maria Teresa and Minerva are arraigned and sentenced to five years in prison at a "joke of a trial," with no representation.

The OAS (Organization of American States) is coming to investigate the political prisoners' situation, and Minerva urges Maria Teresa to share the incident she has written down with the OAS. Rumors spread through the prisoner community that Leandro is accused of being a traitor, and Maria Teresa worries that "The movement is falling apart with all this mistrust and gossip." Meanwhile, Dinorah is bothering the rest of the cellmates even more than usual. When Patria slips Maria Teresa a newspaper clipping reporting that the OAS is actually coming to investigate, she smuggles it out of the visiting room by braiding it into her hair. The guards are nervous that the prisoners might complain, and Maria Teresa feels bad for Santiclo.

On July 11, Maria Teresa tells Magdalena's heartbreaking story: as a young girl, she worked as a maid for a wealthy family, the de la Torres, and was repeatedly raped there. She became pregnant, and the Dona threw her out. She gave birth to Amantina, but the de la Torres took her away from her mother. When Magdalena tried to get her back, breaking into the home with a knife, she was sentenced to 20 years in prison for attempted murder. After telling the story, Magdalena kisses Maria Teresa, making her feel uncomfortable.

The OAS Peace Committee will be interviewing one prisoner from each pavilion, and the head guards choose Maria Teresa. Because the rooms will be tapped and she will not be able to speak aloud freely, Minerva tries to persuade her to smuggle in to them a personal statement about what she went through in La 40, along with a letter explaining what their conditions are *really* like. After her ten-minute session in the visitors' hall with seven members of the committee, Maria Teresa lets the letter containing the statement written by Minerva and Sina and signed "The Fourteenth of June Movement" fall out of her braid, and the young commissioner leading her out picks it up. However, she does not let drop the letter with her own personal account.

On August 7, Maria Teresa reports that she and Minerva will be released the next day along with the other women politicals. She feels sad to be leaving Magdalena behind; the other female inmates seem to have become her sisters. They have a little going away party.

Analysis

In this chapter, Maria Teresa includes little asides in parentheses. When she discusses how most of the women break down and cry, she explains, "The alternative is freezing yourself up, never showing what you're feeling, never letting on what you're thinking. (Like Dinorah. Jailface, the girls call her.)" In reporting the second time she was questioned: "they didn't even threaten that much except to say that it was too bad a pretty lady would have to grow old in prison. Miss out on ... (A bunch of lewd comments I won't bother to repeat here.)" The whole diary is secret and must be hidden from guards, and the inclusion of these little parenthetical notes reflects the secrecy of the whole chapter.

Maria Teresa uses rhetorical questions throughout the chapter. Though the whole chapter is, obviously, Maria Teresa's narration, it is as if these sections are a special window into the questions she asks herself without speaking aloud: "And it's certain now—Leandro is not here with the rest of us. Oh God, where could he be?" In some cases, rhetorical questions are asked inside parentheses, as if Maria Teresa is including them only as an aside to the line of narrative: "[Minerva] says we don't want to create a class system in our cell, the haves and have nots. (We don't? What about when Tiny gave Dinorah a *dulce de leche* as payment for her favors, and she didn't offer anyone a crumb, even Miguelito?)."

The symbol of thread appears again in this chapter, when Maria Teresa is discussing with Magdalena the connection between people. They decide, "There *is* something deeper. Sometimes I really feel it in here, especially late at night, a current going among us, like an invisible needle stitching us together into the glorious, free nation we are becoming."

Maria Teresa's style of punctuating her diary narrative with exclamations continues throughout this chapter. After her arraignment, she writes the date: "Wednesday, May 25 (125 days - 1,826 days to go - Oh, God!)." The next entry, she records, "Wednesday, June 15 (I've decided to stop counting - it's just too depressing!)." She has found out that she and Minerva are each sentenced to five years, and though Minerva's reaction is to laugh, Maria Teresa's is to cry. In commenting on the new women guards who are appointed to "impress the OAS with the prison system's delicacy towards women prisoners," Maria Teresa exclaims, "Delicacy! These women are as tough or tougher than the men."

Though the intimate bond between Minerva and Maria Teresa that has been developing throughout the novel is made clear in this chapter, Maria Teresa decides to go against her sister's wishes and does not give the OAS the letter of her personal account. She explains, "The second note with my story was lodged further up in my braid. Maybe it was the sight of that ribbon Santiclo had given me when I was so broken, I don't know. But right then and there, I decided not to drop the second note. I just couldn't take a chance and hurt my friend." This decision demonstrates an important difference between Maria Teresa and Minerva: Minerva tells her little sister, "This isn't personal, Mate ... This is principle," but Maria Teresa sees Santiclo as more than just a symbol of what they are revolting against; she sees him as a person, and she refuses to risk his being punished or even shot.

Summary and Analysis of Part III - Chapter Twelve: Minerva, August to November 25, 1960

House Arrest, August and September

Minerva and Maria Teresa have been released to house arrest; Minerva struggles to adjust to all the stimuli of Mama's house and finds herself overwhelmed. To make money, they start up a specialty business of making children's christening gowns. They are allowed to visit their husbands at La Victoria on Thursdays and to attend church on Sundays. But when she goes out, Minerva feels overwhelmed by all the people wanting to see her and wish her well, since she has become famous.

Minerva survives by putting on "that hardest of all performances, being my old self again," though she feels frail. Though at first she hides from Captain Pena when he comes to visit, eventually she has to face him. He suggests that they write a thank you letter to Trujillo, so that maybe he will visit their province. Though the other sisters want to write it, Minerva is against it. She is not convinced until Patria points out that it might help save Leandro, Manolo, and Pedrito, who are still in jail. That night, the spies who constantly lurk outside their home are being loud on the porch, and Minerva goes outside to reprimand them.

Elsa Sanchez, Minerva's old friend from school, has married Roberto Suarez, and although they support the revolution, they are not involved in the movement. They pick up radio news on their boat and visit Minerva at the house to report what they have heard. One day, Elsa reports that the OAS has imposed sanctions. That Thursday as they prepare to visit their husbands, Dede warns them that they are putting themselves in danger by traveling all together.

At the prison, Manolo is depressed and tells Minerva to find out who is left in their movement in the area. But a few days later, Elsa brings news that a group of young men has been caught distributing revolutionary leaflets in Santiago. Trujillo is cracking down out of panic, and Captain Pena reports that the women can no longer visit their husbands at La Victoria until the end of September. When they do return to the prison, Manolo believes that he and the other political prisoners are going to be killed, and he tells Minerva, "It's over for us." This adversity reawakens the revolutionary spirit inside Minerva, and she decides, "The butterflies were not about to give up!"

Saving the Men, October

Rufino, the girls' favorite driver, takes them to visit Delia Santos, one of their ex-fellow prisoners who also is a doctor. In truth, Minerva asks her who in their area is still involved in the revolution. Delia reports that Sina has sought asylum, but she writes the name of Dr. Pedro Vinas, a urologist in Santiago, on a sheet of paper for Minerva to see, in case the office is being spied upon. Captain Pena is furious that they went to visit Delia, but Patria explains that it was about "women's problems." They also ask his permission to visit Dr. Pedro Vinas, and he grants it.

Minerva goes to visit Dr. Pena, and he explains the disaster that was the failed uprising. He hopes to let the "gringos" bring Trujillo down, so then the people can take over. But when Minerva reports this news to Manolo, he worries that the gringos will take over the revolution first and the country afterward. Manolo's mother, Dona Fefita, is there, too, and she tearfully tells Minerva that she has arranged to buy their little house to have for them when Manolo gets out of prison, but she adds that he told her he was not coming home alive, so not to bother.

Dona Fefita does not have a chance to buy the house; Minerva receives a note to remove her possessions from the house in Monte Cristi. Dede accompanies her there, but on the way they are stopped by the police. When they are asked to identify themselves, Dede says she is Minerva. But at the police station in Monte Cristi, Minerva identifies herself as herself and shows her pass from Captain Pena.

Dede helps Minerva organize and clean out her old house. In the early evening, Minerva goes to the door and sees a huge crowd of people there to see her, all dressed in black. They return to Chea Mirabal's house on Wednesday, and Tio Pepe tells them that he has just come from a reception honoring Trujillo at the mayor's house. He overheard Trujillo say, looking straight at him, "My only two problems are the damn church and the Mirabal sisters." The next Thursday on the way to La Victoria to visit their husbands, they stop at SIM headquarters as usual. But Pena tells them that Manolo and Leandro are being transferred to Puerto Plata, nearer to where the sisters live.

Talk of the People, Voice of God, November 25, 1960

On November 25, on the way to Puerto Plata, Rufino decides to stop and pick up a young soldier who is hitchhiking. Maria Teresa is nervous about it, but Patria thinks they will be safer with him in the car with them, and Minerva makes small talk with him. The young soldier does not know who they are, but he reports that two politicals, Manolo and Leandro, were admitted last month but are going to be moved back to the capital in a few weeks. It begins to rain hard, but Rufino wants to keep driving. That morning, before they left, Dede had begged them not to all travel together, but they had ignored her.

The sisters stop at a store called El Gallo on the way to Puerto Plata to buy sewing supplies for their company. They decide to buy purses, too. But the salesclerk, Jorge Almonte, recognizes them and puts his card in Minerva's purse. As they drive past La Cumbre, they see Captain Pena's car parked there, and they realize there must be an ambush up ahead. This is corroborated by the card Jorge Almonte slipped Minerva, on which he has written, "Avoid the pass." But there is nothing to be done, so they keep driving.

Minerva suspects the young soldier is a plant, so she begins to interrogate him. They make it safely to Puerto Plata without stopping. They visit Leandro and Manolo, who asks Minerva not to drive back that night but to wait until the next day, saying, "Please, *mi amor*. There are too many rumors around." On the way out of town, they stop at a little restaurant/gas pump for refreshments. Minerva tries to call Chea Mirabal's house phone, but the line is busy. They decide to head home.

Analysis

In Chapter 10, Patria compared Captain Pena to the devil, but now that he has maneuvered things so that Minerva and Maria Teresa could be released from prison, he is compared to God. Since their five-year sentence has been commuted to house arrest, "we had only a few rules to obey. (We called them Pena's commandments)." This is a reference to the Ten Commandments, part of the fundamental law of Christianity traditionally revealed to Moses by God.

While Minerva compares Captain Pena to God in that he hands down commandments, she also breaks from the theme of comparing Trujillo to God and instead compares him to the devil. When the spies at Mama's house call out, "Viva Trujillo!" she balks, thinking, "I wasn't going to invoke the devil's name in my own yard." Tio Pepe voices this opinion as well when he tells the girls about the reception in Trujillo's honor that was held at the mayor's house, calling the dictator a "devil in human form."

Dede becomes nervous about all of her sisters traveling together to visit their husbands, and her warnings serve as foreshadowing for their deaths. When they laugh at her warnings and she gets upset, Minerva says, "Come on, Dede. Think how sorry you'd be if something should happen to us and you didn't say goodbye." But before they leave, she cries out her real fear: "I don't want to have to live without you." The reader knows that is her fate exactly: to live after her sisters die as martyrs, and thus to tell their story. Another instance of foreshadowing occurs after Tio Pepe reports what Trujillo said at the gathering at the mayor's house. Minerva thinks, "As we stood in the dark a while longer, calming ourselves, I had this eerie feeling that we were already dead and looking longingly at the house where our children were growing up without us."

The idea of life as woven of thread appears yet again in this chapter, as Minerva tries to get her old self back: "And so the struggle with her began. The struggle to get my old self back from her. Late in the night, I'd lie in bed, thinking, You must gather up the broken threads and tie them together." She is trying to reinvigorate the "calm, courageous companera" whom Manolo married. They also keep their lives together by literally using thread in their dressmaking business: "We couldn't sleep nights, so we sewed. Sometimes Patria started a rosary, and we all joined in, stitching and praying so as not to let our minds roam."

The theme of courage also emerges through Dede. She is so worried for the safety of her sisters that she becomes angry at them for traveling to visit their husbands all together. However, when she and Minerva are pulled over by the police on their way to Monte Cristi, Minerva can see the terror on her face, but still she identifies herself as Minerva Mirabal in order to protect her little sister.

Authoritarianism is a theme that runs throughout the novel, embodied by the Trujillo regime and its police, laws, and spies. The theme is obvious to the citizens throughout their lives under this regime in the Dominican Republic. Here, it is evident when Minerva and Dede are brought into the police station in Monte Cristi. When Minerva mentions that Captain Pena has given them permission to travel there, with a veiled threat to the officer who is questioning them, "The paroxysm of blinking made me pity the poor man. His own terror was a window that opened onto the rotten weakness at the heart of Trujillo's system." Though Minerva calls the fear instilled in all the officers of the authoritarian regime a "weakness," it is what holds the regime in power.

Summary and Analysis of Epilogue

Through the stories of visitors who come to visit her after her sisters' deaths, Dede is able to piece together the events of the afternoon on which they died. They left the town of Puerto Plata after 4:30; she learns about their stop at the restaurant/gas pump from the proprietor and his wife; she learns about their drive up the mountain from the passengers of a Jeep that left the restaurant/gas pump at about the same time as they did. The sisters were witnessed being apprehended and taken away "peaceably" in a blue and white Austin, but Patria yelled, "Tell the Mirabal family in Salcedo that the *calies* are going to kill us!"

After "Trujillo was gone," the trial of the murderers was on TV for a month, and they admitted to killing the Mirabal sisters and Rufino by strangulation. Then they put them back in the Jeep and pushed it over the edge of a cliff at 7:30 at night. This part of the story was reported to Dede by Mateo Nunez, who traveled all the way from his "remote mountain shack" just to tell her what he knew about her sisters' death. Although the murderers were sentenced to long terms, "all of them were set free during our spell of revolutions." Manolo, Leandro, and Pedrito are all released, and Trujillo is assassinated. Jaimito tries to tell Dede about it, but she prefers not to read the newspapers.

On the night of her sisters' murder, Dede hasn't slept at all because Jaime David is up sick. A messenger comes to her house summoning her to Chea Mirabal's house. When she and Jaimito get there the house is in chaos, and Mama says, "Tell me it isn't true." She has received a telegram reporting that there has been a car accident, and the telegram asks them to go to the hospital in Santiago. This gives Dede hope since it means that her sisters could be still alive, just injured.

After Dede and Mama pack a bag to bring to the hospital, however, they receive the news that the girls are dead. They drive the bodies of the girls and Rufino home from the morgue slowly, with Dede standing in the back of the pick-up with the coffins. As they pass the SIM post, Dede yells, "Assassins!" at it. Jaimito has to gun the motor so she is not heard and killed as well. When she says that she would rather be dead with her sisters, he tells her, "This is *your* martyrdom, Dede, to be alive without them."

After Manolo is released from prison, he regrets losing the argument with Minerva about whether the girls should stay in Puerto Plata for the night. He becomes famous, and Leandro stays by his side until he goes up into the mountains trying to rally the people "when it all came down a second time." They accept amnesty, but they are shot when they come down from the mountains. Manolo has sent a seashell to his daughter Minou, but Dede does not give it to her until she finally asks directly, "Is Papi dead?"

Finally, back in 1994, Minou has her own baby, Camila, whom she tells Dede all about. She suggests that Dede refuse to welcome any more visitors with questions, and that she record the story and sell it instead. Over supper with her friend Olga, Dede discusses how she is living in the past. She tells Olga, "I'm not stuck in the past, I've just brought it with me into the present." That night, she overhears a conversation between Minou and her husband, Doroteo, and is reminded of Minerva and Manolo.

Dede goes over a list of the things and people she has lost throughout her life, including Jaimito and Mama. Afterward, she sums up, "The complete list of losses. There they are. And it helps, I've found, if I can count them off, so to speak." She ran into Lio and his wife at a reception in honor of her sisters, and they caught up intensely about the past. She remembers this as she stands overhearing the conversation between Minou and Doroteo, then goes inside to tuck Minou in. Then she falls asleep herself, but it is different that night; she does not hear the spirits of her sisters running through the house. Instead, "all I hear is my own breathing and the blessed silence of those cool, clear nights under the anacahuita tree before anyone breathes a word of the future."

Analysis

All of the previous chapters titled "Dede" have not actually been from Dede's point of view; rather, they have been from the third person point of view with Dede as the main character. However, in the epilogue she is the narrator for the first time. It is as if by reconnecting with her sisters through telling the woman interviewer their stories, she has been able to reconnect with herself. This revival of the young girl inside her results in her first person narrative, in which she is able to come to terms with her actions and decisions regarding the revolution.

The role of women has changed by 1994, and Dede realizes this change through her niece Minou, who has designed a line of play clothes for her store in the capital while she teaches courses at the university on poetry and politics. In fact, all of the next generation of her family, including Manolito, are "smart young men and women making good money. They aren't like us, I think. They knew almost from the start they had to take on the world." The men and women are unified in this way, rather than divided by their traditional roles.

The theme of entrapment is apparent once again in Dede's reaction to the telegram Mama shows her on the morning after the girls' death. When they receive the telegram and think that the girls might be alive, "my heart in my rib cage was a bird that suddenly began to sing. Hope!" This metaphor extends the conceit of a cage around the whole island of the Dominican Republic, taking it inward, to the personal level. Dede has been trapped by her own fear (or conversely, she keeps her heart safe inside the cage of her own soul), and the telegram gives her a bit of short-lived hope; the caged bird sings.

Dede receives the seashell Manolo sends to Minou but decides not to give it to Minou right away, keeping her father's death a secret from her. This decision is reminiscent of her decision to burn Lio's letter to Minerva, Minou's mother, instead of delivering the invitation to come away with him. At this point in her life, Dede is still making other people's decisions for them, deciding to protect people from the recklessness of those who love them.

In the epilogue, it is revealed indirectly that Dede has had a breast removed due to cancer. This absence on her body preoccupies her, and it also symbolizes the absence of her family and all those she has lost. It is also one more loss to count on the list. When she compares Minou to Minerva in her mind, "absently, my hand travels to my foam breast and presses gently, worrying an absence there." While she worries about not hearing the spirits of her sisters running about through the house as she falls asleep, "my hand worries the absence on my left side, a habitual gesture now. My pledge of allegiance, I call it, to all that is missing." For Dede, so much of her story is a story of loss, but in finally telling so much of the story this time, in honoring their memory, she has stilled, at least momentarily, the ghosts of those she has lost.

.

Suggested Essay Questions

1. **What is the purpose of Alvarez's use of violent imagery?**

   The violent imagery that permeates the entire novel demonstrates the constant presence of Trujillo in his authoritarian regime, with a constant threat of violence everywhere. It is apparent already in the first chapter, as Enrique Mirabal jokes about how quickly he had four daughters: "Bang-bang-bang, their father likes to joke, aiming a finger pistol at each one, as if he were shooting them, not boasting about having sired them." The joke is about their births, so the foreshadowing of their deaths is ironic. During the ill-fated centennial performance, when Ramfis jumps up to grab the bow from the approaching Sinita before she reaches his father Trujillo, he moves "quick as gunfire." Violent diction is particularly significant in Chapter 6: as Enrique Mirabal leads Minerva down the driveway into the garden, "The moon was a thin, bright machete cutting its way through patches of clouds." This metaphor is continued when Minerva describes its light as "sharp," foreshadowing the slap she is about to receive from her father.

2. **How does Alvarez address becoming a woman?**

   In Chapter 2, the title of the section "Complications" refers both to Minerva's becoming a woman physically, since this is the euphemism Sor Milagros uses for menstruation, and to growing up emotionally as she learns about Trujillo's evil for the first time the night she begins to menstruate. Maturation involves developing a more critical eye regarding oneself and one's leaders and authority figures. The two forms of growing up are linked with a simile; as Minerva listens to Sinita's story, "the aching in my belly was like wash being wrung so tightly, there wasn't a drop of water left in the clothes." Patria observes her daughter, Noris, becoming a woman in Chapter 8. When Noris meets her after the mountainside is bombed, Patria notices "a change in her, as if her soul had at last matured and begun its cycles." This imagery recollects Chapter 2, in which Minerva begins her "complications" both physically and emotionally as she realizes the country is in danger, and the power and evil of Trujillo. It also is reminiscent of Maria Teresa, who in her diary entries as a young girl yearned to discover her soul.

3. **How does the theme of entrapment symbolize the authoritarian regime in the Dominican Republic?**

   The dire situation of the Dominican Republic is particularly apparent through the symbol of a cage. When Minerva describes wanting to leave home to go to school, she considers herself trapped at home, and she views going to Inmaculada Concepcion as a kind of escape. She sees her own situation mirrored in that of the rabbits in their pens, but she realizes that she is nothing like a rabbit when the rabbit that she tries to let free refuses to leave the cage. As for her, "I'd just left a small cage to go into a bigger one, the size of our whole country." In the epilogue, the theme of entrapment is apparent in Dede's reaction to the telegram Mama shows her on the morning after the girls' death. It says that there has been a car accident and that they should go to the hospital in Santiago, meaning that the girls might be alive. "And my heart in my rib cage was a bird that suddenly began to sing. Hope!" The conceit of a cage can be applied to the whole island of the Dominican Republic or to one's personal feelings. Dede has been trapped by her own fear, and the telegram gives her a bit of short-lived hope. There is also something safe and protective about a cage—regardless of the regime, thoughts are free inside oneself—and militarily, the revolutionaries from other countries are at first repelled by the Dominican Republic's protective forces. Thus, perhaps the rabbit demonstrates some wisdom in choosing to remain entrapped and safe from harm. Yet, the difference with Trujillo's regime is that the cage door is not open; there is not a choice.

4. **Describe the relationship between Maria Teresa and Minerva.**

Maria Teresa's devotion to and admiration of Minerva is apparent throughout her diary entries. After all, it is Minerva who gave her both her first and her second diaries, encouraging her to reflect as a way to "deepen one's soul." She demonstrates her commitment to Minerva by lying for her, corroborating her story that their Tio Mon is ill, to protect Minerva after she has been caught sneaking out of school. In lying for Minerva, Maria Teresa becomes involved in her older sister's revolutionary activities indirectly. It is the beginning of their downfall, and this is expressed as a simile of jumping into water together.

The reader also learns about many important events in Minerva's life through Maria Teresa's diary entries. For instance, we learn in Maria Teresa's report about the speech at Salcedo Civic Hall that Minerva has gained permission to attend law school. We also learn about Minerva's marriage to Manolo, the birth of Minou, and Trujillo's denial of her license to practice law upon graduation from law school.

The symbol of thread appears in this chapter, when Maria Teresa is discussing the connection between people with Magdalena. They decide, "There is something deeper. Sometimes I really feel it in here, especially late at night, a current going among us, like an invisible needle stitching us together into the glorious, free nation we are becoming." Being stitched together does not mean they are the same, however. When she finds out that she and Minerva are each sentenced to five years, Minerva's reaction is to laugh, but Maria Teresa's is to cry.

In Chapter 11, Maria Teresa decides to go against her sister's wishes and does not give the OAS the letter of her personal account. She explains, "The second note with my story was lodged further up in my braid. Maybe it was the sight of that ribbon Santiclo had given me when I was so broken, [but] I just couldn't take a chance and hurt my friend." This decision demonstrates an important difference between Maria Teresa and Minerva: Minerva tells her little sister, "This isn't personal, Mate ... This is principle," but Maria Teresa sees Santiclo as more than just a symbol of what they are revolting against, because she sees him as a person and refuses to risk his being punished or even shot.

5. **How is the weather used to reflect the narrative?**

When Sor Asuncion calls in Patria to have a talk about listening for her calling from God, the storm that Patria sees brewing outside is a metaphor for her earthly calling, at odds with her desire to be a nun: "I could see just outside the window the brilliant red flames lit in every tree, and beyond, some threatening thunderclouds." When Sor Asuncion tells her to pray to the Virgencita for guidance, she "saw the first zigzag of lightning, and heard, far off, the rumble of thunder." She takes it as a hint that she is not meant to become a nun. As Patria prays with Sor Asuncion, she remembers, "I tried hard but I could not keep my eyes from straying to the flame trees, their blossoms tumbling in the wind of the coming storm."

The ominous events of the Discovery Day party are also mirrored by the weather's progression to a rain storm. When they arrive at the party, "there is a strong breeze, announcing rain." When Minerva mentions Lio's name, "suspicion clouds the gaze" of Trujillo's face; and when she refuses to dance with Manuel de Moya initially, "a cloud of annoyance crosses his face." When Minerva slaps Trujillo, it is like the clap of thunder that begins the storm: "and then the rain comes down hard, slapping sheets of it." In the midst of the storm, her family is the ship that steers her to temporary safety: "Dede and Patria are turning in all directions like lookouts on the mast of a ship."

6. **How does Patria's view of Trujillo as like God change?**

Throughout the novel, Patria compares Trujillo to God, specifically Jesus. In Chapter 4, while Patria lies beside Minerva in the hammock, they look at the pictures of Jesus and El Jefe hung side by side. Minerva notes, "They're a pair, aren't they?" This inspires Patria to question why God would allow their country to suffer so at the hands to Trujillo. When she looks up to challenge the picture of Jesus, "the two faces had merged!" This experience points out the Godlike role that Trujillo plays; he is omniscient, with his spies, penetrating everyone in the country, making almost everyone into his "disciples" or spies. In Chapter 10, Patria says, "Maybe because I was used to the Good Shepherd and Trujillo side by side in the old house, I caught myself praying a little greeting as I walked by." She wants her family back from him, and "prayer was the only way I knew to ask."

But when Patria arrives at the capital for the release of Nelson, she feels no kinship toward him—quite the opposite: "The more I tried to concentrate on the good side of him, the more I saw a vain, greedy, unredeemed creature. Maybe the evil one had become flesh like Jesus!"

7. **How are traditional views of women challenged in the novel?**

The theme of the role of women emerges for Patria in Chapter 4, as she worries about Minerva getting worked up about the government. She says to her little sister, "It's a dirty business, you're right. That's why we women shouldn't get involved." But Minerva argues "that women had to come out of the dark ages." Speaking to the interview woman, Dede addresses the theme of the role of women. She says, "'Back in those days, we women followed our husbands.' Such a silly excuse. After all, look at Minerva. 'Let's put it this way,' Dede adds. 'I followed my husband. I didn't get involved.'" She is aware that she was using the traditional female role as an excuse for not supporting her sisters, something for which she still feels guilty.

8. **How does Lio Morales affect the relationship between Dede and Minerva?**

There has always been tenseness between Dede and Minerva. Their personalities are at odds: Minerva is full of questions and mischief, while Dede is much more organized and chooses to smile and dismiss things without stirring up trouble. But it is Lio who brings out Dede's resentment toward her sister. Though she loves Jaimito, Dede is jealous of Lio's interest in Minerva. She sees them as a glamorous couple doing exciting things, while she and Jaimito are expected to end up together. She exposes them hiding in the bushes together, and she even burns Lio's letter intended for her sister. Dede tells herself it is to protect Minerva, but it is clearly also borne of jealousy that her sister might get involved in such a daring adventure with Lio.

9. **Describe how Alvarez creates the feeling that death is lurking in Maria Teresa's diary entries.**

Death seems to lurk throughout Chapter 7 in particular. Of course, Enrique Mirabal has actually died, and Maria Teresa's recurring dream revolves around a coffin. But she also uses language that calls death to mind; the chapter opens with her statement, "I feel like dying myself!" When she comes back to her diary on July 3, she writes, "Diary, I know you have probably thought me dead all these months."

10. **How is Patria tied both to heaven and to earth?**

As narrator, Patria uses similes and personification that connect her both to heaven and to earth. For a while she is torn between becoming a nun and becoming a woman focused on earthly matters. When Padre de Jesus tells her he cannot help her because he, too, is lost, she says, "I was shaking like when a breeze blows through the sacristy and the votive candles flicker." She is in the position of the prayerful candles, being shaken by nature. When she is overwhelmed by the beauty of Constanza, she personifies the land and nature as if it is tied to God: "Purple mountains reaching towards angelfeather clouds; a falcon soaring in a calm blue sky; God combing His sunshine fingers through green pastures straight out of the Psalms." Pedrito ties Patria to earth. She is attracted to him for his animal-like qualities, and when he proposes to her he pours dirt into her hand. This is also evident in the language she uses to express how she is not worried about him like she worries about her sisters: "Pedrito didn't worry me. I knew he would always have one hand in the soil and the other somewhere on me."

Patria's struggle to reconcile heaven and earth comes to a climax in Chapter 9 as she breaks down on Mama's front lawn. She tears up the grass from the ground around her, screaming. Dede gets down on her knees and puts the ground back in place, and "in a soothing voice, she reminded her sister of the faith that had always sustained her." Dede leads Patria in reciting the Credo, helping her find refuge in heaven when Pedrito, who connects her to earth, has been taken from her.

Fourteenth of June Movement

Julia Alvarez fictionalizes and retells the true story of the Mirabal sisters and their role in the revolutionary activities that eventually led to the overthrow of the Trujillo regime in the Dominican Republic. Indeed the sisters had enough popularity in the country that after they were reported to have been murdered by the regime in 1960, the rising revolutionary ferment boiled over until Trujillo himself was assassinated about six months later (about two years after the June 14, 1959, invasion discussed below). Inside the revolutionary movement, the sisters were known as the "butterflies" because this was Minerva's codename. The particular part of the movement involving the Mirabal sisters, Manolo, and other characters in the novel became known as the Fourteenth of June Movement.

The revolutionary impulse had already existed prior to June 14, 1959, when armed revolutionaries from outside the country were repelled by the regime, but this conflict is what gave the Mirabal sisters' movement its name. Almost exactly ten years earlier, on June 19, 1949, exiled Dominicans had tried to overthrow Trujillo's dictatorship by landing on Luperón bay by Puerto Plata, but they had failed. In 1959, another attempt to topple the regime was launched from Cuba. (Internet sources are rather unreliable, sometimes conflating the 1949 and 1959 events, and sometimes conflating the 1959 invaders with the later Fourteenth of June domestic revolutionary group.)

In a May 5, 1959, FBI record (<u>FBI record 2-1423-9TH NR 36</u>), it was reported that "During the past few days we have received information from three substantial sources that invasion of Cuba from Dominican Republic is imminent. The sources are: (1) General Manuel Benitez, head of National Police of Cuba from 1940 to 1944 and member of Cuban Legislature from 1948 to 1958; (2) Frank Perez Perez, a source of Miami Office who is aligned with General Benitez and Rolando Masferrer, former Cuban Senator and newspaperman who maintained a private army of hoodlums while Batista was in power and who has been described as a bandit and gangster; (3) I. Irving Davidson, registered agent of Israeli and Nicaraguan Governments who talked with Batista in the Dominican Republic on 4/29/59 and who quotes Batista as stating a group of Cuban riffraff is planning invasion of Cuba from the Dominican Republic with approval of Generalissimo Trujillo who feels Castro will attack if not attacked first."

Castro did help a revolutionary force attack first, about a month later. The attack on June 14 and June 20, 1959, came on three fronts, by both land and sea. Richard Lee Turits in *Foundations of Despotism* reports that the fighters were Dominican exiles and other revolutionaries from Cuba and elsewhere in Latin America. These members of the Dominican Liberation Movement had trained in Cuba for about three months. The air landing in Constanza, in the middle of the country, involved several dozen rebels. They were dressed in Dominican Air Force uniforms and fought Trujillo's forces in the nearby mountains.

On July 6, 1959, *Time Magazine* <u>reported</u>: "'If aggressors want to see their beards and brains flying **like butterflies**, let them approach the shores of the Dominican Republic,' warned Dictator Rafael Leonidas Trujillo. A pair of Cuba-based rebel invasion forces—one of 63 men arriving by C46 at the mountain-ringed, mid-island town of Constanza, and another of 150 aboard two Chris-Craft launches that landed near Puerto Plata on the north coast—put the strongman's boast to the test of arms. Last week, both by government and rebel account, Trujillo proved that he meant what he said." (emphasis added)

Indeed, as for the Puerto Plata attack, Turits argues that they maintained loyalty to the regime and chose to defend it rather than help the rebels. Turits notes that the peasants of other, disaffected areas, such as Monte Plata, might have been more likely to help. As *Time* reported, "the government countered rebel claims of a successful landing with a communiqué full of gore. The 'liberators' who survived an air and naval bombardment, it said, 'waded ashore apparently hoping still to march on Ciudad Trujillo with the aid of peasants. It did not work that way. Machete-swinging farmers beat government troops to the beach. The invasion ended in a murderous flailing of razor-sharp machetes on the reddened sands. Army patrols found only dismembered bodies.'"

Trujillo used the occasion to start <u>modernizing his military capabilities</u>, and he awarded <u>medals</u> to the successful soldiers which read, "Constanza Heroismo y Lealtad." Cuba ended diplomatic relations with the Dominican Republic and tried to drum up United Nations support for the rebels.

As for the domestic revolutionaries, the failed invasion had a catalyzing effect. The <u>revolutionary group in Puerto Plata</u>, led by Manolo Tavarez Justo and Minerva Mirabal Reyes, gave themselves the name "El Movimiento 14 de Junio" or "The Fourteenth of June Movement," or "J14" for short. While the peasants of Puerto Plata had failed to help the invading forces as expected, Turits notes that the revolutionaries consisted mainly of the country's new middle class of young professionals and merchants, as well as university students. The movement was, understandably, banned, and the assassination of its leaders only caused more and more revolutionary ferment in the country.

Author of ClassicNote and Sources

Meghan Joyce, author of ClassicNote. Completed on July 29, 2009, copyright held by GradeSaver.

Updated and revised Adam Kissel November 15, 2009. Copyright held by GradeSaver.

Julia Alvarez. In the Time of the Butterflies. New York: Penguin Group, 1994.

Silvio Sirias. Julia Alvarez: A Critical Companion. Westport, CT: Greenwood Press, 2001.

Richard Lee Turits. Foundations of Despotism: Peasants, the Trujillo Regime, and Modernity in Dominican History. Stanford: Stanford University Press, 2002.

Bridget Kevane. Latin Literature in America. Westport, CT: Greenwood Press, 2003.

Raysa E. Amador Gomez-Quintero and Mireya Perez Bustillo. The Female Body: Perspectives of Latin American Artists. Westport, CT: Greenwood Press, 2002.

Bridget Kevane. Profane and Sacred: Latino/a American Writers Reveal the Interplay of the Secular and the Religious. Westport, CT: Greenwood Press, 2007.

Julia Alvarez. "Julia Alvarez." 2009-07-09. 2009-07-09.
<http://www.juliaalvarez.com/>.

Secretaría de Estado de Cultura, Archivo General de la Nacíon, Dominican Republic. "El Movimiento 14 de Junio en Puerto Plata." 2008-10-21. 2009-11-15.
<http://www.agn.gov.do/departamentos-agn-dominicana/dep-hemeroteca-biblioteca/historia-d

Essay: Minerva's Struggle

by Anonymous
October 06, 2001

Although this is an era when violence is frowned upon and war deplored, still the soldier has remained an esteemed figure. Even more appealing to the imagination are tales of tyrants and the courage of the underground guerillas that oppose them. Such almost mythic status has been conferred upon three sisters, nicknamed the Butterflies, who participated in the fight against the thirty-year dictatorship of Rafael Leonidas Trujillo in the Dominican Republic. While heroic deeds take the spotlight, one may forget that even freedom fighters begin as children. That they learn as children and grow as humans, fallibly and inconstantly, is a fact remembered by Dominican novelist Julia Alvarez. In Alvarez's novel In the Time of the Butterflies, she uses several turning points in the life of Minerva Mirabal to define that character's growth as a human being rather than a hero.

Alvarez uses two turning points in Minerva's childhood to show her potential for the life ahead of her, yet emphasize her childish innocence. In the beginning of the novel, Alvarez introduces Minerva to the reader with Minerva's excitement that her Pap plans to send her away to school. School becomes Minerva's first victory and step towards her life as a revolutionary fighter. This, Minerva says, "[i]s how I got free" (13). Alvarez uses Minerva's departure for school and her excitement for it to signify Minerva's early emotional divorce from the need for her parents' approval and dependence on their value system, while demonstrating with this scene how independent and strong-minded Minerva is, as compared especially to her sisters. At school, Minerva experiences a prelude to what may be the biggest turning point in her life. For all her independence, she still believes in the propaganda that Trujillo and his administration have spread. Her good friend Sinita tells Minerva a story of Trujillo's evil as they whisper under blankets late at night like the schoolgirls they are. Minerva says to Sinita, " 'Bad things?...Trujillo was doing bad things?' It was as if I had just heard Jesus had slapped a baby" (17). Although Minerva does not fully accept the image of Trujillo as a tyrant, when she wakes up the next morning she finds that she has received her first period; Alvarez has made her a woman. When Trujillo seduces a classmate named Lina, she comes to realize his corruption, if not with the maturity of an adult, saying, "I felt sorry for him. Pobrecito! At night, he probably had nightmare after nightmare like I did, just thinking about what he'd done (24). Alvarez illustrates Minerva's childlike faith in a world where guilt accompanies sin, and to such an extent as to draw pity. Here Alvarez places her in a position from which she may step into her new role as a rebel, while also demonstrating that she is currently too young for such responsibility.

As Minerva grows older, Alvarez uses Minerva's impulsiveness to allow her to realize her own strength. Minerva confronts Pap after finding that he has fathered illegitimate children, and "saw his shoulders droop...right then and there, it hit me harder than his slap: I was much stronger than Pap...He was the weakest one of all" (89). Alvarez led Minerva to discover her power by her own actions in order to justify her portrayal of the character as drawing strength from herself while also giving it to those around her. Minerva's energy and conviction in herself and in her cause carries her into a role in the underground and then into and through La 40, a prison. Alvarez shows Minerva's strength there through the admiring, if sullen, eyes of her younger sister and comrade, Mara Teresa, who, after crying, says, "Lord forbid Minerva should see me, or she'd give me another one of her talks about morale" (233). Minerva has assumed a motherly role in the uprising. However, after Trujillo grants Minerva and her sister release and puts them under house arrest, Minerva's spirit takes a turn for the worse. She says, "[I was] shocked at what I was letting happen to me. I had been so much stronger and braver in prison. Now at home I was falling apart" (258). Her bravery becomes little more than a performance, and Alvarez emphasizes the change with the many acquaintances who lean close to Minerva to whisper, "Vivan las Mariposas!" Although many still look to Minerva for leadership and strength, she is not always able to provide it for herself.

Alvarez, while she does not flinch from showing Minerva's faults, also does not deprive the girl of the more heroic standing she has built towards. She does not allow Minerva to wallow in her sorrow for much longer, and another turning point comes when she and her sisters fear than their husbands will be executed. Minerva reflects that "By now in my life I should have known. Adversity was like a key in the lock for me. As I began to work to get our men out of prison, it was the old Minerva I set free" (269). The challenge gives Minerva reason to rise again. Although, due to the fact that she is tightly guarded, Minerva never again reaches the level of political activity she had as a free woman, she and her sisters do begin to investigate the state of their old underground once more. That Minerva's spirit is whole and healthy again is clearly demonstrated by Alvarez near the very closing of the book. Even as Minerva and her sisters travel towards what appears to be an ambush, Minerva feels an air of excitement. She ventures, "I don't know quite how to say this, but it was as if we were girls again, walking through the dark part of the yard, a little afraid, a little excited by our fears, anticipation the lighted house just around the bend - That's the way I felt as we started up the first mountain" (297). Although Alvarez reports that Minerva felt excited as she and her sisters "started up the first mountain," in reality, most of Minerva's mountains have already been crossed. She begins as a naive child, encounters injustice, fights it, becomes depressed, and then after all this rights herself. Alvarez conveys through this that Minerva's resurrection, while not the most revered of her acts or the one that earned her the love of her country, may be her most heroic stage of life; a hero must not only overcome threats to her country but threats to her spirit.

Alvarez reveals the theme that a few people, while they may not cause an entire revolution, can provide inspiration and motivation for others. While the Butterfly sisters represent this motif of bravery for the Dominican Republic, Minerva likewise represents it for her family. Although each sister has her own inner strength, only Minerva has enough to both fortify herself and sustain others. She passes though many stages of life in the novel as her country's political situation develops. Although it is ironic in the traditional sense of a hero's unassailable person that both Minerva and her foe Trujillo are eventually brought down, and she much sooner than he, it is consistent with Alvarez's depiction of Minerva as not a traditional hero, but a woman.

Essay: The signficance of flight and migration in Caribbean literature

by Julio D. Rodriguez
March 08, 2006

Significance of Flight and Migration in Caribbean Literature

One of the most recurring themes throughout most of Caribbean literature are those of flight and migration. The existence of these themes in Caribbean literature is a result of hundreds of years of slavery. They are significant in that they, to the writer, represent escape from oppression, be it psychological and or physical. This is to be expected since most people in the Caribbean come from slave decent. Although slavery was abolished over 100 years ago, it is still significant to those who ancestors experienced it. Writers like Julia Alvarez, Jean Rhys, Olive Senior, and E.A. Markham have all made huge contributions to Caribbean literature. Pieces such as Alvarez's In the Time of the Butterflies, Rhys' Wide Sargasso Sea, Senior's over the roofs of the world, and Markham's The Sea will allow us to further analyze the significance of flight and migration throughout the literature of the Caribbean.

Rhys' Wide Sargasso Sea deals with a Creole woman, Antoinette, who battles in finding her identity. Being a Creole during this time was not easy. The native people did not accept many of them and neither did the colonialists. Not quite English and not quite native, Antoinette struggles with these two sides in defining herself. Like a bird, Antoinette is caged by this struggle. We see this struggle in her when she is telling Rochester about Amelie calling her a "white cockroach". "So between you I often wonder who I am and where is my country and where do I belong and why was I ever born at all." (Sargasso Sea, p. 61) There is a deep struggle and longing to belong to something. Some may argue that this is one of the reasons she marries Rochester, but the truth is that she is constantly plagued by this and feels lost. Trapped in her struggle she longs to take flight/migrate to a place where she thinks she may belong. Since she doesn't feel accepted by the natives, she feels that maybe she will be accepted by her Englishmen. "I have been too unhappy, I thought, it cannot last, being so unhappy, it would kill you. I will be a different person when I live in England and different things will happen to me...England, rosy pink in the geography book map..." (Sargasso Sea, p. 66) To Antoinette this is her escape, her migration to a better life. She feels that she will become an entirely different person in England that she can finally escape from her cage of struggle.

Alvarez's In the Time of the Butterflies really allows us to see how significant the themes of flight and migration are. In this novel we meet Mirabal sisters or as they are sometimes called "the Butterflies". These four sisters lived in a time when oppression was the basis of their countries government and policy. Although they are living in a state of political oppression, they are also oppressed because they were women. We can really this when Minerva explains "And that's how I got free. I don't mean just going to sleep away school on a train with a trunkful of new things. I mean in my head after to Inmaculada and met Sinita and saw what happened to Lina and realized that I'd just left a small cage to go into a bigger one, the size of our country"(Butterflies, p.13) When Minerva arrives at Inmaculada she goes through an awakening. She was never exposed to or even heard of the atrocities of Trujillo until then. She was a caged bird in her home because of her sex, but now that she has learned about the current state of her country she realizes that she is in fact still caged. Minerva being the most strong-minded and self willed of all her sisters, she takes it upon herself to take "flight" and free herself.

When we think of flight and migration, we think of the motion of an object through the air, maybe even transcending the earth. In many ways these "Butterflies" do transcend by breaking through the barriers and limits set for them as both women and citizens of the Dominican Republic during the era of Trujillo. Patria's description of the way she felt during her retreat to the mountains foreshadows the time of transcendence to come for her, her church, and her sister Dede. "My old yearning to be in the religious life stirred. I felt myself rising, light-headed with transcendence, an overflowing fountain" (Butterflies, p. 160) Alvarez is keen in that she foreshadows the awakening that will finally occur in Patria and Dede. During this same retreat Patria experiences for the first time the effects of Trujillo's oppression, a dead boy in her hands about the same age as her daughter Noris. "Coming down that mountain, I was a changed woman. I may have worn the same sweet face, but now I was carrying not just my child but the dead boy as well" (Butterflies, p. 162) This event has changed Patria drastically. Not only does Patria carry her own burdens, but she is also now ready to carry that of the struggle. Alvarez allows us to see the internal change that occurs in Patria. She transcends from a woman who is weary of giving her self to a cause or even her own calling because of the choices she has made in her life to be married and to have children, to a woman who is now not only carrying her own burdens but is now willing and able to carry the burden of the struggle, a burden she was never courageous enough to take on until now.

Over the roof of the world is a collection of poems by Olive Senior that uses nature as a model and a metaphor for life in the Caribbean. As we read the first few poems from this collection we can't escape the recurring themes of birds and flight. She uses birds to represent the native people of the Caribbean and their capture by and struggle against colonialism. Senior is allowing us to see that, like birds, her people in the Caribbean have been captured and caged. The titles of her poems also allude to this, The Secret of Capturing Parrot and The Secret of Taming Parrot. Flight is also another of the recurring themes in this collection. "For you, flight is given as gift of bird messenger sustained by rattle, by drum, by song. You soar, sail, glide." (Roofs, p. 17) From this we can make the connection that, like birds, Caribbean natives have been given the gift of flight, the gift to escape the colonial cages. Supported by rattles, drums, and songs, flight depends on the endowed's personal expression of freedom, his/her ability to soar and glide through treacherous of weather and migrate.

E. A. Markham is Caribbean born poet that has lived who immigrated to England in 1956. The Sea is a poem that deals with his perception of the sea at two separate points in his life. The Sea is a medium by which everything moves in the Caribbean. It is a medium for which both the good and the bad enter the islands. According to Markham it has brought "white ships and news of a far land" (Sea, p.199), but it has also brought the oppression and unwelcome control of colonialism to the islands. The role of the Sea in the Caribbean fluctuates between two extremes, life and destruction. It brings life because from it natives receive food and sustenance, but it can also bring destruction in the form of hurricanes, not to mention colonialism and its devastating effect on Caribbean life and culture. The sea was, during this time, the only way a native could migrate outside of the islands. So, not only does it provide food, as well as destruction, the sea now provides the only escape Caribbean natives had to escape colonialism in their land. Towards the end of the poem, Markham tells us that "Today, I have visitors. They come long distances overland. They will be uneasy and console me for the loss of the sea. I will discourage them." (Sea, p.199) In this passage we again encounter the theme of migration and escape from colonialism. He is telling us that after his migration to England he really has no reason to long for or crave the sea. To him, all that the sea could provide was a medium by which he could migrate to England and now that he has done so, he doesn't yearn for it.

Throughout most of Caribbean literature we see themes of flight and migration; themes that is essence symbolize escape. This should not be a surprise to anyone because all of the Caribbean countries and colonies were built on slavery. It has in someway even become part of their culture. Regardless of how many years have passed since slavery, or how many Caribbean writers use them in their works, the themes of flight and migration will continue resound in the hearts of many natives because the effects of slavery are still being felt today.

Essay: The signficance of flight and migration in Caribbean literature

Quiz 1

1. **What is the anniversary of the death of the Mirabal sisters?**
   A. April 30th
   B. August 1st
   C. December 20th
   D. November 25th

2. **What kind of tree is at the end of the road to the Mirabal house?**
   A. Orange
   B. Oak
   C. Anacahuita
   D. Roble

3. **In 1994, what is Dede's job?**
   A. Teacher
   B. Interview woman for a news station
   C. Life insurance salesperson
   D. Dressmaker

4. **Who claims to be able to communicate with the dead Mirabal sisters?**
   A. The interview woman
   B. Dede
   C. Fela
   D. Minou

5. **What is Patria's career goal when she is growing up?**
   A. Trujillo's mistress
   B. Teacher
   C. Nun
   D. Housewife

6. **Whose father, uncles, and brother have been killed by Trujillo's regime?**
   A. Padre de Jesus
   B. Sinita
   C. Elsa
   D. Sor Milagros

7. **Who becomes one of Trujillo's mistresses?**
    A. Sinita
    B. Lourdes
    C. Elsa
    D. Lina Lovaton

8. **What is NOT the name of of one of Patria's children?**
    A. Nelson
    B. Minou
    C. Noris
    D. Raul Ernesto

9. **Who gives Maria Teresa her first diary?**
    A. Patria
    B. Minerva
    C. Enrique Mirabal
    D. Sor Milagros

10. **Who is NOT one of Maria Teresa's cousins?**
    A. Manolo
    B. Jaimito
    C. Raul
    D. Berto

11. **Where does Minerva sneak out of Inmaculada Concepcion to go?**
    A. Home to take care of Mama
    B. An affair with Trujillo
    C. Secret meetings at Don Horacio's house
    D. Visiting Tio Mon, who is ill

12. **Where does Patria meet Pedrito for the first time?**
    A. While she is washing his feet at the church
    B. At Inmaculada Concepcion
    C. At the Discovery Day dance
    D. On the road to Monte Cristi

13. **What news comes out during the Mirabal women's pilgrimage to Higuey?**
    A. Maria Teresa is engaged
    B. Papa is having an affair
    C. Patria is pregnant again
    D. Manolo is having an affair

14. **Which man creates a romantic rift between Dede and Minerva?**
    A. Manolo
    B. Jaimito
    C. Enrique Mirabal
    D. Lio Morales

15. **What do Dede and Minerva often do at Tio Pepe's house?**
    A. Play volleyball
    B. Have secret meetings with revolutionaries
    C. Organize the shop
    D. Daydream about law school

16. **Where does Jaimito propose to Dede?**
    A. At a revolutionary meeting
    B. In Enrique Mirabal's Ford
    C. On the beach
    D. In the garden

17. **Who burns a letter from Lio to Minerva?**
    A. Jaimito
    B. Enrique Mirabal
    C. Dede
    D. Maria Teresa

18. **Who discovers Carmen and Enrique Mirabal's illegitimate family?**
    A. Patria
    B. Minerva
    C. Dede
    D. Maria Teresa

19. **Where does Minerva find letters to her from Lio?**
    A. In the pocket of Papa's dress jacket
    B. In Dede's jewelery box
    C. At Carmen's house
    D. At Tio Pepe's house

20. **Who is Manuel de Moya?**
    A. A guard at La Victoria prison
    B. The Mirabals' revolutionary cousin
    C. Enrique Mirabal's best friend
    D. Trujillo's secretary of state

21. **Who slaps Trujillo at the Discovery Day dance?**
    A. Patria
    B. Sinita
    C. Minerva
    D. Mama

22. **Who knew Trujillo during their early days in the military?**
    A. Ramfis
    B. Tio Pepe
    C. Enrique Mirabal
    D. Tio Chiche

23. **What does Minerva use to bet Trujillo in his office?**
    A. Loaded dice
    B. The weather
    C. A coin
    D. An hourglass

24. **Who does NOT attend Papa's funeral?**
    A. Manolo
    B. Margarita
    C. Maria Teresa
    D. Carmen

25. **What is in the recurring nightmare that Maria Teresa has?**
    A. A coffin
    B. A thread
    C. Trujillo's palace
    D. A ship

Quiz 1 Answer Key

1. **(D)** November 25th
2. **(C)** Anacahuita
3. **(C)** Life insurance salesperson
4. **(C)** Fela
5. **(C)** Nun
6. **(B)** Sinita
7. **(D)** Lina Lovaton
8. **(B)** Minou
9. **(B)** Minerva
10. **(A)** Manolo
11. **(C)** Secret meetings at Don Horacio's house
12. **(A)** While she is washing his feet at the church
13. **(B)** Papa is having an affair
14. **(D)** Lio Morales
15. **(A)** Play volleyball
16. **(B)** In Enrique Mirabal's Ford
17. **(C)** Dede
18. **(B)** Minerva
19. **(A)** In the pocket of Papa's dress jacket
20. **(D)** Trujillo's secretary of state
21. **(C)** Minerva
22. **(D)** Tio Chiche
23. **(A)** Loaded dice
24. **(A)** Manolo
25. **(A)** A coffin

Quiz 2

1. **Who betrays the Mirabal family by spying on them?**
   A. Tia Flor
   B. Fela
   C. Raul
   D. Prieto the yardboy

2. **What does Minerva study at the capital?**
   A. Religion
   B. Law
   C. Philosophy and Letters
   D. Forensics

3. **Who is Palomino?**
   A. Manolo
   B. Leandro
   C. Jaimito
   D. Pedrito

4. **What news does Patria receive from Minerva, Manolo, Leandro, and Nelson on New Year's Eve?**
   A. Nelson is joining the underground revolution
   B. The Cuban revolution has succeeded
   C. She is pregnant
   D. The first wave of liberators has arrived in the Dominican Republic

5. **Where does Patria go while she is pregnant with Raul Ernesto?**
   A. To stay at Chea Mirabal's home
   B. On retreat with the Christian Cultural Group
   C. On vacation with Pedrito
   D. To stay with Minerva and Manolo in Monte Cristi

6. **Which religious person is NOT a revolutionary?**
   A. Padre de Jesus
   B. Brother Daniel
   C. Sor Asuncion
   D. Padre Gabriel

7. **Why does Pedrito hesitate to let the revolutionaries meet at his home?**
   A. Because he is suspicious of Padre de Jesus
   B. Because he does not want Nelson to get involved in the movement
   C. Because he is preparing to leave Patria
   D. Because he could lose his land for helping them

8. **In 1994, why is Minou emotional when she returns from Fela's?**
   A. She is afraid she is pregnant again
   B. Fela said the dead Mirabal sisters would not come to talk to her
   C. Dede has breast cancer
   D. Fela is going crazy

9. **What does Dede decide after her sisters ask her to join the underground movement?**
   A. That she will leave Jaimito
   B. That she will do whatever it takes to save her marriage
   C. That she will join the church
   D. That she will start her own revolutionary movement

10. **What is wrong with Dona Belen?**
    A. She has breast cancer
    B. She is unable to have children
    C. She has lost a leg in a bomb attack
    D. She is old and probably suffers from dementia

11. **Why does Dede panic and leave the rectory?**
    A. She has forgotten her purse
    B. She does not want to travel with Dona Belen
    C. She realizes Padre de Jesus is a revolutionary
    D. She realizes Jaimito has left her

12. **Who suggests that Dede and Jaimito fix their marital problems by taking a vacation together?**
    A. Manolo
    B. Minerva
    C. Dona Leila
    D. Mama

13. **Why do Pedrito and Nelson come down from the hills and give themselves up to the SIM?**
    A. They see bombings happening on the other side of the hill
    B. They see the SIM holding a gun to Patria's head
    C. They see their house being burned down
    D. They hear a radio report from Cuba

14. **What does Minerva suffer from?**
    A. Breast cancer
    B. Tuberculosis
    C. Dementia
    D. Depression

15. **Who is head of the northern division of the SIM?**
    A. Manuel de Moya
    B. Nelson
    C. Enrique Mirabal
    D. Captain Pena

16. **Who is the last to be taken to prison?**
    A. Nelson
    B. Minerva
    C. Pedrito
    D. Maria Teresa

17. **Who does Patria begin to pray to, along with Jesus?**
    A. Pedrito
    B. Trujillo
    C. Papa
    D. Captain Pena

18. **When the SIM makes Pedrito an offer of freedom, what do they say he must give up?**
    A. His land
    B. His marriage to Patria
    C. His house
    D. His children

19. **How does Padre Gabriel surprise Patria?**
    A. By giving a revolutionary sermon
    B. By locking the congregation in the church
    C. By forming an underground cell
    D. By allowing her to bury weapons on church land

20. **What is NOT an example of how Trujillo's regime lashes out against the church?**
    A. By sending prostitutes to church
    B. By declaring Catholicism as treason
    C. By attempting to assassinate the archbishop during Mass
    D. By putting the latrine's contents inside the church

21. **Who delivers a letter from Maria Teresa in prision to Patria and Mama?**
    A. Margarita
    B. Papa
    C. Captain Pena
    D. Carmen

22. **Where does Margarita work?**
    A. In a whorehouse
    B. In a doctor's office
    C. In a pharmacy
    D. In the jail as a guard

23. **Which of the following does Patria and Chea NOT send Minerva and Maria Teresa in prison?**
    A. A new diary
    B. Underwear
    C. A comb
    D. A black towel

24. **Who drives Patria to Captain Pena's office?**
    A. Dede and Jaimito
    B. Dona Belen
    C. Mama
    D. Don Bernardo

25. **Who takes Patria and Pedrito's land?**
    A. Manuel de Moya
    B. Enrique Mirabal
    C. Tio Chiche
    D. Captain Pena

Quiz 2 Answer Key

1. **(D)** Prieto the yardboy
2. **(B)** Law
3. **(B)** Leandro
4. **(B)** The Cuban revolution has succeeded
5. **(B)** On retreat with the Christian Cultural Group
6. **(C)** Sor Asuncion
7. **(D)** Because he could lose his land for helping them
8. **(B)** Fela said the dead Mirabal sisters would not come to talk to her
9. **(A)** That she will leave Jaimito
10. **(D)** She is old and probably suffers from dementia
11. **(C)** She realizes Padre de Jesus is a revolutionary
12. **(A)** Manolo
13. **(B)** They see the SIM holding a gun to Patria's head
14. **(B)** Tuberculosis
15. **(D)** Captain Pena
16. **(D)** Maria Teresa
17. **(B)** Trujillo
18. **(B)** His marriage to Patria
19. **(A)** By giving a revolutionary sermon
20. **(B)** By declaring Catholicism as treason
21. **(A)** Margarita
22. **(C)** In a pharmacy
23. **(A)** A new diary
24. **(D)** Don Bernardo
25. **(D)** Captain Pena

Quiz 3

1. **Who is pardoned and released from prison first?**
   A. Manolo
   B. Nelson
   C. Minerva
   D. Pedrito

2. **What does Patria offer to give Captain Pena when Nelson comes home?**
   A. Her land
   B. Sex
   C. A sancocho
   D. Money

3. **Who does NOT go to the capital to pick Nelson up when he is released from prison?**
   A. Patria
   B. Padre de Jesus
   C. Tio Chiche
   D. Noris

4. **Who is Santiclo?**
   A. A guard at La Victoria
   B. A friend of the Mirabal family
   C. Minerva and Manolo's landlord
   D. A professor at the university

5. **Who is NOT one of Minerva and Maria Teresa's cell mates at La Victoria?**
   A. Patria
   B. Dinorah
   C. Magdalena
   D. Sina

6. **Who tries to kiss Maria Teresa on the mouth while she is in prison?**
   A. Dinorah
   B. Pedrito
   C. Magdalena
   D. Sina

7. **Who is deaf?**
    A. Balbina
    B. Santiclo
    C. Magdalena
    D. Delia

8. **Who is a doctor?**
    A. Sinita Perozo
    B. Balbina
    C. Elsa Sanchez
    D. Delia Santos

9. **What do the prisoners wear as a sign of solidarity?**
    A. Little crucifix necklaces
    B. Special rings
    C. Pink bras
    D. Matching underwear

10. **Who is the first person Maria Teresa tells about the events that happened to her in La 40?**
    A. Patria
    B. Minerva
    C. Magdalena
    D. Delia

11. **How does Maria Teresa slip the OAS the letter signed by The Fourteenth of June Movement?**
    A. She hides it in her food
    B. She puts it in her diary
    C. She lets it fall out of her braid
    D. Through Santiclo

12. **Why do the guards start treating Minerva, Maria Teresa, and the other prisoners a little better?**
    A. Trujillo feels bad for the political prisoners
    B. They have become revolutionaries
    C. The OAS is coming to investigate and they are scared
    D. They are physically scared of the women's collective power

13. **How does the SIM convince Leandro to do a job for Trujillo?**
    A. By torturing him
    B. By taking his land
    C. By putting him in solitary confinement
    D. By torturing Maria Teresa in front of him

14. **After being released from prison, why does Minerva have to stay in the house?**
    A. Because she is depressed and the sun bothers her
    B. Because she is on house arrest
    C. Because she is pregnant
    D. Because Minou is ill and needs her care

15. **How do Elsa and Roberto Suarez keep up to date on the news about the revolution?**
    A. By listening to the radio from their boat
    B. From Fidel Castro
    C. From Minerva
    D. From the notes Maria Teresa drops from her braid

16. **Who is the sisters' favorite driver?**
    A. Rufino
    B. Pedrito
    C. Enrique Mirabal
    D. Don Bernardo

17. **Who does Delia Santos tell Minerva to see?**
    A. Dr. Pedro Vinas
    B. Dinorah
    C. Manolo in prison
    D. Her mother

18. **What type of business do the Mirabal women start when Minerva and Maria Teresa get back from prison?**
    A. Alcohol
    B. Letter-writing
    C. Marijuana
    D. Dressmaking

19. **What type of doctor is Dr. Vinas?**
    A. Pediatrician
    B. Dentist
    C. Urologist
    D. Ob-Gyn

20. **Why does Manolo tell Dona Fefita not to buy his and Minerva's house?**
    A. He wants to divorce Minerva
    B. He knows she cannot afford it
    C. He is convinced he is going to die in prision
    D. It is bugged

21. **Who accompanies Minerva to clean out her house in Monte Cristi?**
    A. Patria
    B. Manolo
    C. Dede
    D. Maria Teresa

22. **In Maria Teresa's recurring nightmare, which of the following is NEVER in the coffin?**
    A. Manolo
    B. Leandro
    C. Mama
    D. Papa

23. **Who reports the news that Trujillo has said, "My only two problems are the damn church and the Mirabal sisters"?**
    A. Tio Pepe
    B. Minerva
    C. Tio Chiche
    D. Captain Pena

24. **What is the name of the prison where Minerva and Maria Teresa are kept?**
    A. Inmaculada Concepcion
    B. La 40
    C. La Victoria
    D. The OAS

25. **Where are Manolo, Pedrito, and Leandro transferred after Minerva and Maria Teresa are released from prison?**
    A. San Francisco
    B. La 40
    C. La Victoria
    D. Puerto Plata

Quiz 3 Answer Key

1. **(B)** Nelson
2. **(C)** A sancocho
3. **(B)** Padre de Jesus
4. **(A)** A guard at La Victoria
5. **(A)** Patria
6. **(C)** Magdalena
7. **(A)** Balbina
8. **(D)** Delia Santos
9. **(A)** Little crucifix necklaces
10. **(C)** Magdalena
11. **(C)** She lets it fall out of her braid
12. **(C)** The OAS is coming to investigate and they are scared
13. **(D)** By torturing Maria Teresa in front of him
14. **(B)** Because she is on house arrest
15. **(A)** By listening to the radio from their boat
16. **(A)** Rufino
17. **(A)** Dr. Pedro Vinas
18. **(D)** Dressmaking
19. **(C)** Urologist
20. **(C)** He is convinced he is going to die in prison
21. **(C)** Dede
22. **(C)** Mama
23. **(A)** Tio Pepe
24. **(C)** La Victoria
25. **(D)** Puerto Plata

Quiz 4

1. **Who do the girls and Rufino pick up on the side of the road on their way to Puerto Plata?**
   A. Nelson
   B. Trujillo's son Ramfis
   C. Pedrito
   D. The young soldier

2. **What do the Mirabal sisters buy on their way to Puerto Plata?**
   A. Snacks
   B. Gasoline
   C. New purses
   D. Shoes for their husbands

3. **How does Jorge Almonte warn Minerva?**
   A. By sending her a hidden message on the radio
   B. By hiding a note in Maria Teresa's braid
   C. By whispering in her ear
   D. By writing a note on his business card

4. **Who does Minerva try to call from the restaurant/gas pump on the way home from Puerto Plata?**
   A. Patria
   B. Manolo
   C. Rudy and Pilar
   D. Mama

5. **What does the first telegram delivered to Mama's house about the fate of her dead daughters say?**
   A. Rufino has kidnapped her daughters
   B. There has been a car accident and she should come to the hospital
   C. They have been murdered
   D. Her daughters have been apprehended for contraband

6. **On the ride back from the morgue with the girls' dead bodies, who rides in the back with the coffins?**
   A. Nelson
   B. Jaimito
   C. Dede
   D. Minou

7. **What disease does Dede suffer from later in life?**
    A. Breast cancer
    B. Drug addiction
    C. Skin cancer
    D. HIV/AIDS

8. **What part of her body does Dede lose?**
    A. A finger
    B. A breast
    C. A kidney
    D. An eye

9. **What does Manolo give to Dede to deliver to Minou on the day he dies?**
    A. A seashell
    B. One of Minerva's sweaters
    C. A long letter
    D. A radio

10. **Who is Olga?**
    A. A doctor who used to be involved in the revolution
    B. One of Dede's friends as an adult
    C. One of Minerva's old classmates
    D. Lio Morale's new wife

11. **Which of the following dies last?**
    A. Manolo
    B. Minerva Mirabal
    C. Enrique Mirabal
    D. Chea Mirabal

12. **Where does Dede meet Lio close to 1994?**
    A. At his new house near the old presidential palace
    B. At a reception in honor of her sisters
    C. At her mother's home
    D. On the road to Puerto Plata

13. **Where does Dede want to travel next in 1994?**
    A. The United States of America
    B. Canada to see the leaves
    C. Cuba
    D. Spain

14. **Who introduces Minerva and Dede to Lio?**
    A. Patria
    B. Tio Pepe
    C. Enrique Mirabal
    D. Mario

15. **What does Pedrito put in Patria's hand when he proposes to her?**
    A. A bundle of money
    B. Dirt
    C. A small bird
    D. A ring

16. **Who is captured by the SIM after hiding at Inmaculada Concepcion?**
    A. Minerva
    B. Don Horacio
    C. Hilda
    D. Sor Asuncion

17. **Who tries to shoot Trujillo during a recitation performance?**
    A. Manolo
    B. Sinita Perozo
    C. Minerva Mirabal
    D. Elsa Sanchez

18. **Who has been a colonel in the army since the age of four?**
    A. Ramfis
    B. Trujillo
    C. Tio Chiche
    D. Captain Pena

19. Why does Maria Teresa have to bury her first diary?

A. Because she writes down Leandro's codename

B. Because she sketches plans of nipple bombs

C. Because she mentions Hilda's name in it

D. Because she mentions being the head of a revolutionary cell

20. What does Maria Teresa suffer from even as a young girl?

A. Asthma

B. Depression

C. Polio

D. Cancer

21. Whose coffin does Patria have a couple of campesinos dig up?

A. Her baby after a miscarriage

B. Pedrito

C. Enrique Mirabal

D. Lio Morales

22. Who never works as a servant for any of the Mirabals?

A. Tinita

B. Fela

C. Tono

D. Captain Pena

23. Who cannot read or write?

A. Enrique Mirabal

B. Margarita

C. Chea Mirabal

D. Maria Teresa

24. Who seeks political asylum?

A. Tio Pepe

B. Minerva

C. Enrique Mirabal

D. Lio Morales

25. **What does Minerva tell her father when he hits her in the garden?**
    A. That he has lost her respect
    B. That she knows about his illegitimate family
    C. That she wants to go to Trujillo's party
    D. That Mama deserves better

Quiz 4 Answer Key

1. **(D)** The young soldier
2. **(C)** New purses
3. **(D)** By writing a note on his business card
4. **(D)** Mama
5. **(B)** There has been a car accident and she should come to the hospital
6. **(C)** Dede
7. **(A)** Breast cancer
8. **(B)** A breast
9. **(A)** A seashell
10. **(B)** One of Dede's friends as an adult
11. **(D)** Chea Mirabal
12. **(B)** At a reception in honor of her sisters
13. **(B)** Canada to see the leaves
14. **(D)** Mario
15. **(B)** Dirt
16. **(C)** Hilda
17. **(B)** Sinita Perozo
18. **(A)** Ramfis
19. **(C)** Because she mentions Hilda's name in it
20. **(A)** Asthma
21. **(A)** Her baby after a miscarriage
22. **(D)** Captain Pena
23. **(C)** Chea Mirabal
24. **(D)** Lio Morales
25. **(A)** That he has lost her respect

Quiz 5

1. **Who of the following is NOT a landlady to any of the Mirabal sisters?**
   A. Dona Hita
   B. Dona Belen
   C. Dona Isabel
   D. Dona Chelito

Quiz 5 Answer Key

1. **(B)** Dona Belen

ClassicNotes

GradeSaver™

Getting you the grade since 1999™

Other ClassicNotes from GradeSaver™

1984
Absalom, Absalom
Adam Bede
The Adventures of Augie
   March
The Adventures of
   Huckleberry Finn
The Adventures of Tom
   Sawyer
The Aeneid
Agamemnon
The Age of Innocence
The Alchemist (Coelho)
The Alchemist (Jonson)
Alice in Wonderland
All My Sons
All Quiet on the Western
   Front
All the King's Men
All the Pretty Horses
The Ambassadors
American Beauty
Angela's Ashes
Animal Farm
Anna Karenina
Anthem
Antigone
Antony and Cleopatra
Aristotle's Ethics
Aristotle's Poetics
Aristotle's Politics
As I Lay Dying
As You Like It
Astrophil and Stella
Atlas Shrugged
The Awakening

Babbitt
The Bacchae
Bartleby the Scrivener
The Bean Trees
The Bell Jar
Beloved
Benito Cereno
Beowulf
Bhagavad-Gita
Billy Budd
Black Boy
Bleak House
Bless Me, Ultima
Blindness
The Bloody Chamber
Bluest Eye
The Bonfire of the
   Vanities
The Book of the Duchess
   and Other Poems
Brave New World
Breakfast at Tiffany's
Breakfast of Champions
The Brothers Karamazov
The Burning Plain and
   Other Stories
A Burnt-Out Case
By Night in Chile
Call of the Wild
Candide
The Canterbury Tales
Cat on a Hot Tin Roof
Cat's Cradle
Catch-22
The Catcher in the Rye

The Caucasian Chalk
   Circle
Charlotte's Web
The Cherry Orchard
The Chocolate War
The Chosen
A Christmas Carol
Christopher Marlowe's
   Poems
Chronicle of a Death
   Foretold
Civil Disobedience
Civilization and Its
   Discontents
A Clockwork Orange
The Color of Water
The Color Purple
Comedy of Errors
Communist Manifesto
A Confederacy of
   Dunces
Confessions
Connecticut Yankee in
   King Arthur's Court
The Consolation of
   Philosophy
Coriolanus
The Count of Monte
   Cristo
Crime and Punishment
The Crucible
Cry, the Beloved
   Country
The Crying of Lot 49
Cymbeline
Daisy Miller

For our full list of over 250 Study Guides, Quizzes,
Sample College Application Essays, Literature Essays and E-texts, visit:

www.gradesaver.com

ClassicNotes

GrⱯdeSaver™

Getting you the grade since 1999™

Other ClassicNotes from GradeSaver™

David Copperfield
Death in Venice
Death of a Salesman
The Death of Ivan Ilych
Democracy in America
Devil in a Blue Dress
Dharma Bums
The Diary of a Young
  Girl by Anne Frank
Disgrace
Divine Comedy-I:
  Inferno
Doctor Faustus
  (Marlowe)
A Doll's House
Don Quixote Book I
Don Quixote Book II
Dora: An Analysis of a
  Case of Hysteria
Dr. Jekyll and Mr. Hyde
Dracula
Dubliners
East of Eden
Electra by Sophocles
The Electric Kool-Aid
  Acid Test
Emily Dickinson's
  Collected Poems
Emma
Ender's Game
Endgame
The English Patient
Ethan Frome
The Eumenides
Everything is Illuminated
Fahrenheit 451

The Fall of the House of
  Usher
A Farewell to Arms
The Federalist Papers
For Whom the Bell Tolls
The Fountainhead
Frankenstein
Franny and Zooey
The Glass Menagerie
The God of Small Things
The Good Earth
The Grapes of Wrath
Great Expectations
The Great Gatsby
The Guest
Gulliver's Travels
Hamlet
The Handmaid's Tale
Hard Times
Harry Potter and the
  Philosopher's Stone
Heart of Darkness
Hedda Gabler
Henry IV (Pirandello)
Henry IV Part 1
Henry IV Part 2
Henry V
Herzog
The Hobbit
Homo Faber
House of Mirth
The House of the Seven
  Gables
The House of the Spirits
House on Mango Street
Howards End

A Hunger Artist
I Know Why the Caged
  Bird Sings
I, Claudius
An Ideal Husband
Iliad
The Importance of Being
  Earnest
In Cold Blood
In Our Time
In the Time of the
  Butterflies
Inherit the Wind
Invisible Man
The Island of Dr. Moreau
Jane Eyre
Jazz
The Jew of Malta
The Joy Luck Club
Julius Caesar
Jungle of Cities
Kama Sutra
Kidnapped
King Lear
The Kite Runner
Last of the Mohicans
The Legend of Sleepy
  Hollow
Leviathan
Libation Bearers
Life is Beautiful
Life of Pi
Light In August
The Lion, the Witch and
  the Wardrobe
Lolita

For our full list of over 250 Study Guides, Quizzes,
Sample College Application Essays, Literature Essays and E-texts, visit:

www.gradesaver.com

ClassicNotes

GrdeSaver™

Getting you the grade since 1999™

Other ClassicNotes from GradeSaver™

Long Day's Journey Into
    Night
Lord Jim
Lord of the Flies
The Lord of the Rings:
    The Fellowship of the
    Ring
The Lord of the Rings:
    The Return of the
    King
The Lord of the Rings:
    The Two Towers
A Lost Lady
The Lottery and Other
    Stories
Love in the Time of
    Cholera
The Love Song of J.
    Alfred Prufrock
Lucy
Macbeth
Madame Bovary
Manhattan Transfer
Mansfield Park
The Master and
    Margarita
MAUS
The Mayor of
    Casterbridge
Measure for Measure
Medea
Merchant of Venice
Metamorphoses
The Metamorphosis
Middlemarch

A Midsummer Night's
    Dream
Moby Dick
Moll Flanders
Mother Courage and Her
    Children
Mrs. Dalloway
Much Ado About
    Nothing
My Antonia
Mythology
Native Son
Nickel and Dimed: On
    (Not) Getting By in
    America
Night
Nine Stories
No Exit
Notes from Underground
O Pioneers
The Odyssey
Oedipus Rex or Oedipus
    the King
Of Mice and Men
The Old Man and the Sea
Oliver Twist
On Liberty
On the Road
One Day in the Life of
    Ivan Denisovich
One Flew Over the
    Cuckoo's Nest
One Hundred Years of
    Solitude
Oroonoko
Othello

Our Town
The Outsiders
Pale Fire
Paradise Lost
A Passage to India
The Pearl
Persuasion
Phaedra
Phaedrus
The Piano Lesson
The Picture of Dorian
    Gray
Poe's Poetry
Poe's Short Stories
Poems of W.B. Yeats:
    The Rose
Poems of W.B. Yeats:
    The Tower
The Poetry of Robert
    Frost
The Poisonwood Bible
Portrait of the Artist as a
    Young Man
Pride and Prejudice
The Prince
Prometheus Bound
Pudd'nhead Wilson
Pygmalion
Rabbit, Run
A Raisin in the Sun
The Real Life of
    Sebastian Knight
The Red Badge of
    Courage
The Remains of the Day
The Republic

For our full list of over 250 Study Guides, Quizzes,
Sample College Application Essays, Literature Essays and E-texts, visit:

www.gradesaver.com

ClassicNotes

GradeSaver™

Getting you the grade since 1999™

Other ClassicNotes from GradeSaver™

Rhinoceros
Richard II
Richard III
The Rime of the Ancient
Mariner
Rip Van Winkle and
Other Stories
The Road
Robinson Crusoe
Roll of Thunder, Hear
My Cry
Romeo and Juliet
A Room of One's Own
A Room With a View
A Rose For Emily - Barn
Burning - Other Short
Stories of William
Faulkner
Rosencrantz and
Guildenstern Are
Dead
Salome
The Scarlet Letter
The Scarlet Pimpernel
The Seagull
The Secret Life of Bees
Secret Sharer
Sense and Sensibility
A Separate Peace
Shakespeare's Sonnets
Shantaram
Siddhartha
Silas Marner
Sir Gawain and the
Green Knight
Sister Carrie

Six Characters in Search
of an Author
Slaughterhouse Five
Snow Falling on Cedars
The Social Contract
Something Wicked This
Way Comes
Song of Roland
Song of Solomon
Sons and Lovers
The Sorrows of Young
Werther
The Sound and the Fury
The Spanish Tragedy
Spring Awakening
The Stranger
A Streetcar Named
Desire
The Sun Also Rises
Tale of Two Cities
The Taming of the Shrew
The Tempest
Tender is the Night
Tess of the D'Urbervilles
Their Eyes Were
Watching God
Things Fall Apart
The Things They Carried
A Thousand Splendid
Suns
The Threepenny Opera
Thus Spoke Zarathustra
The Time Machine
Titus Andronicus
To Build a Fire
To Kill a Mockingbird

To the Lighthouse
Treasure Island
Trifles
Troilus and Cressida
Tropic of Cancer
Tropic of Capricorn
The Turn of the Screw
Twelfth Night
Twilight
Ulysses
Uncle Tom's Cabin
Utopia
A Very Old Man With
Enormous Wings
Villette
The Visit
Volpone
Waiting for Godot
Waiting for Lefty
Walden
Washington Square
The Waste Land
Where the Red Fern
Grows
White Fang
White Noise
White Teeth
Who's Afraid of Virginia
Woolf
Wide Sargasso Sea
Winesburg, Ohio
The Winter's Tale
The Woman Warrior
Wordsworth's Poetical
Works
Woyzeck

For our full list of over 250 Study Guides, Quizzes,
Sample College Application Essays, Literature Essays and E-texts, visit:

www.gradesaver.com